VR / AR Enterprise Insider:

Guidebook for

Virtual Reality and XR

1st Edition

Sky Nite

DEDICATION

This book is dedicated to those who would use their talents to better this world, and the infinite worlds beyond.

CONTENTS

Introduction

"I know kung fu."

In the movie "The Matrix" Neo plugs into a computer program and after a moment opens his eyes, having learned kung fu fighting via virtual training. Although we are not yet at the point of full-brain immersion, today's VR and AR systems immerse us convincingly in the digital realm, allowing us to accelerate our productivity in training and beyond.

The simple truth is this: businesses stand to gain billions of dollars of productivity gains by use of VR and AR in the next decade. The technology available TODAY is capable of this; the core limiting factors are awareness of the technology, access to developers, and design know-how.

My hope is that this book will prepare you for either incorporating VR / AR into your enterprise, or creating VR / AR content. It is the culmination of my research on the subject, as well as six years of experience building and educating in the VR / AR industry.

I have done my best to make the book modular so that if you already know about a certain topic you can just skip to the next section. If you're new to the field of VR / AR, this should serve as a great introduction. If you're a veteran of the industry, this book will act as a summary and hopefully expose you to some ideas you have not considered.

"Chapter 1: Fundamentals" focuses on what VR and AR are, how they work, and important terminology for understanding the tech.

"Chapter 2: Advantages of VR / AR" reveals the unique advantages of VR / AR compared to traditional computer interfaces, and gives examples. "Chapter 3: Case Studies" looks at successful uses of VR / AR in enterprise across a range of companies and industries. "Chapter 4: XR Software Design" gives technical advice about how to create VR / AR software that doesn't make people sick. "Chapter 5: Hardware" explores currently available VR / AR hardware and lists the strengths and weaknesses of each. It also looks at future VR / AR tech likely to be seen within 15 years.

As said by Alex Pentland, MIT professor and author of "Social Physics":

"It is not simply the brightest who have the best ideas; it is those who are best at harvesting ideas from others. It is not only the most determined who drive change; it is those who most fully engage with like-minded people."

In that spirit, here are my ideas ripe for harvesting, which have in turn been harvested from across the industry. I hope you'll use these ideas and the tools of VR / AR to better our world.

CHAPTER 1: FUNDAMENTALS

How do we maximize the rate at which we learn something? This is one of my core life interests, and one of VR / AR's great powers. However, I've found one concept from cognitive theory to be useful above all others. This concept helps explain the structure of this book. This concept is "chunking".

To understand chunking, we must first understand "working memory". Essentially, we have a limited amount of information we can hold in our head at any one time. This is the information our brains hold on a short term basis, as opposed to long term memory. If you're familiar with computer hardware, working memory is like RAM while long term memory is like hard drive storage.

Working memory is fairly limited in what it can hold, and currently believed to be largely genetic in terms of inherent capacity. An example of pushing your working memory to the limit (for most people) would be trying to solve the following math problem in your head without writing anything down (I don't recommend actually trying unless you enjoy math):

21 x 35 x 28 = ?

Chunking is our ability to take pieces of information and compress them into a single piece (chunk), which in turn requires a smaller amount of working memory. You can think of a chunk as a group of information with a shared identity. If you were to try to solve the above equation (21 x 35 x 28), you would probably multiply the first two numbers, then take the result and multiply it by the third number. In that case, you chunk the abstract equation 21 x 35 into a single number that is easier to work with. Have you ever wondered why we use phone numbers with the XXX-XXX-XXXX format? By dividing an abstract number into discrete sections, we are able to chunk 10 numbers into 3 collections.

Another example of chunking is converting the description "opening to a room with a handle that swings on hinges" into the word "door". If I say the word "door", you immediately can infer several properties of a door without clogging up working memory. This allows you to understand more complex sentences like "The man ran through the doorway while singing." Most people would read that sentence and instantly picture it in their minds.

However, what if you came from a tribe on a remote island that didn't use doors or have the concept of singing? To understand the sentence you would have to learn about each concept, and your fresh understanding of the concept would make understanding the full sentence take more time. Similarly, a sentence like "This VR experience induces presence in 20% of the cohort, and sim sickness in 10%" will be hard to understand if you haven't learned VR fundamentals and jargon.

So, my goal for this chapter is to equip you with the knowledge you'll need to read about the VR / AR industry, maximizing the speed you can learn about it.

What is VR / AR / MR / XR?

Immersive computing is one of several names given to the burgeoning Virtual Reality and Augmented Reality markets. Terminology in the industry is still in contention, so what I've written here is my own interpretation based on researching the current state of the field and my own interaction in it.

Virtual Reality (VR)

Virtual Reality (VR) is technology that fully immerses you in a virtual world. In its current form, you put on a headset called a Head Mounted Display (HMD) and can be visually transported to any 3D environment. Because of motion tracking and screen technology combined with stereoscopic 3D, the screen disappears and you are simply *there*. If you've seen the movie "The Matrix" you've seen VR, albeit a very advanced version of it that uses direct-brain tech instead of today's wearable displays.

Today's VR is made up of four main parts: 3D stereoscopy, low latency head tracking, high screen refresh rate, and large field of view. These technologies combine to create Presence, the feeling that you are really inside the virtual world. Some examples of VR headsets are the Oculus Rift, Oculus Quest, Playstation VR, Vive, and Valve Index (I'll speak about hardware in more detail in a later chapter).

Here are some terms we'll be using (which will be explained in more depth later in this chapter):

1. *Presence:* The feeling of being somewhere. Immersion that fools the brain and makes you think you're somewhere that you're not.

2. *Sim Sickness:* A nausea that can result from VR / AR hardware or simulated motion.

3. *Rendering:* The computer processing of 3D images for display on screens.

4. *3D Engine*: Software used to create 3D worlds.

Now for a dive into what makes VR possible.

3D Stereoscopic

We have two eyes. Revolutionary, I know. However, it's important to note that because of our two eyes, we are able to perceive depth. Try playing catch with one eye closed and you'll see a large increase in difficulty. You can still infer depth from the change in environmental image (the ball is getting bigger, so it must be getting closer) but the property of "stereoscopy" is missing.

Stereoscopy is the visual perception of objects located in 3D space, and you need at least two reference points to have it. We have been playing with stereoscopic pictures since 1838. If you've ever been to a theater and watched a 3D movie, you've experienced a stereoscopic image. Instead of regular flat video the movie seems to jump out of the screen.

This stereoscopy is important for VR because it tricks your brain into seeing images how we see them in reality. Even though you are looking at a flat screen in the VR headset, your brain perceives one cohesive image that contains depth.

Displaying stereoscopic images in a VR headset (commonly called an HMD or Head Mounted Display) requires that the source has two reference points that match eye width. So, if you want to capture 3D video that has stereoscopy, you need two cameras about eye-distance apart. This "180 degree 3D video" has become a popular and relatively cheap way to record video for VR. The downside of this is that if the user turns their head, the video edge can be seen and will transition into blackness (or whatever color you've programmed as the background). 360 degree video can be achieved with more cameras, both stereoscopic and not.

However, none of these systems allow you to move your head, something that's always possible with 3D engine generated images (think video game animation). Unfortunately, many new VR filmmakers try to use camera systems that DON'T have stereoscopy. Even though the film surrounds the user, the lack of depth breaks immersion and can cause discomfort (nausea, eye strain, etc). The experience is similar to watching a video on a large dome (a display style that you might see at science museums).

If you are planning to capture real-world video for VR, I would recommend using a capture technique that has stereoscopy. That said, using 3D engine imagery over real-world capture is often a better solution than stereoscopic video, depending on the use-case (we'll talk more about which technology to use for your own projects in a later chapter).

Low Latency High Accuracy (Head) Tracking

So, you have 3D images, but what happens when you turn or move your head? With just stereoscopy, nothing. You turn your head and the image stays stuck to your face. That's not a VR headset, that's a wearable 3D TV (a thing that I'm surprised to find actually exists, and yes it's sub-par according to the reviews).

For VR, if you turn your head, it should feel like you are looking around a virtual environment. The image displayed should change by the same angle you've turned your head at a latency (delay) that isn't perceivable. VR tried to make a consumer push in the 1990s but failed, and a huge reason for this was that turning your head required a noticeable delay for the display (screen) to catch up. This caused a breaking of immersion a large amount of simulation sickness.

Modern technology uses cameras and sensors to track the motion of your head to a sub-millimeter accuracy. Shift your head even a little, and that motion will translate into what you see. For those technically minded, the tracking data determines your rendering viewpoint, ensuring that each new frame is drawn from where you are currently looking.

Head tracking when combined with a high refresh rate display allows the screen to stop being a screen and instead become your current reality.

High Refresh Rate Display

Monitor, display, screen, they're all words for the same thing: the piece of technology that shows you visuals. Video is typically displayed at 24 frames-per-second (fps), which means that 24 separate images are shown to you in a single second. The changing of these images is perceived by our brains as continual motion.

Refresh Rate is the amount of times a display can change in one second, a figure that is measured in Hertz (Hz). You can think of Hz as the frames per second (fps) of a display. The refresh rate of a display refers to the hardware, while the frame rate refers to the software. So, if you had a display that updated 30 times a second, it would be a 30 Hz display. Why might we need a display with more than 24 Hz? Games are typically rendered at 30 or 60 fps because doing so offers a crisper, more responsive experience.

VR displays need an even higher refresh rate, since any conscious or even subconscious disconnect from the real world can cause simulator sickness and break presence. To achieve visuals indistinguishable from reality, you'd need a refresh rate matching that of the human eye. Some people's eyes can perceive frame rates up to 1000 fps and beyond. Luckily, we can avoid sim sickness in the majority of the population with much less than that.

The bare minimum refresh rate for VR headsets is 60 Hz. Showing less than 60 fps dramatically lowers the quality of immersion and makes most people sick just from the reduced frame rate. Most headsets on the market as of early 2020 can do at least 72 Hz, which is comfortable for the majority of people for short times. Some headsets offer 90 Hz and 120 Hz, with each step up in frame rate corresponding with increased smoothness, comfort, and immersion.

Unfortunately there doesn't seem to be any publicly published modern research on the percentage of the population affected by different levels of refresh rate in a VR headset (as of early 2020). It's a hard thing to study since the content displayed in the headset makes a difference, and there are a number of confounding factors such as tracking accuracy and field of view. Additionally, each individual seems to be different, and tolerance can be gained.

One way to test a VR headset's refresh rate is to shake your head quickly back and forth, taking note of the visual artifacts (such as visual smear) or lag that results. Note that the software you are running might not be rendering at the display's Hz, and this head shake test can also reveal this. Programs running at a frame rate below the display's refresh rate will cause sim sickness in people who are susceptible. Inconsistent frame rate in your VR software is the leading preventable cause of sim sickness.

Higher refresh rate is better, but only if you have the computer resources for it. Ideally all headsets would run at 120 Hz, but doing so means that the exact same program running on a 60 Hz display would cost about half the compute time. Because VR headsets use high-resolution screens, increasing frame rate also dramatically increases how many pixels you are rendering. For this reason, headset manufacturers have to strike a balance of trade offs. For example, the Oculus Quest uses a 72 Hz display since it runs completely off a mobile computer, while the Valve Index headset defaults at 90 Hz but can go up to 120 Hz since it plugs into a computer with a powerful graphics card.

Frame Rate Amplification Technology is a key improvement on the software side that can alleviate some of the compute cost of higher frame rates. Oculus uses Asynchronous Spacewarp (yes that's what they call it) to double the frame rate of an app running under the headset's refresh rate. For example, on a 90 Hz display it renders only 45 frames, then uses rotation and positional tracking data to render interpolated (i.e. in between) frames to achieve effectively 90 fps, albeit with minor visual artifacts. With the use of AI and other Frame Rate Amplification Technology, interpolated frames may become the default rendering mode some day (but we're not there yet as of early 2020).

If you want more detail on Frame Rate Amplification, check out: https://www.blurbusters.com/frame-rate-amplification-technologies-frat-more-frame-rate-with-better-graphics/

Large Field of View

Field of view (FOV) is the observable area we can see at any given moment. In an ideal virtual reality headset, the field of view would match that of our eyes. Human eyes have a surprisingly large FOV: about 200 degrees horizontal and 135 degrees vertical when combined. About 120 degrees of your horizontal field of view is seen by both eyes, meaning that you only see stereoscopy (i.e. depth) within that range. The extra 40 degrees of monocular (i.e. single eye) vision on each side is your peripheral vision. Peripheral vision is unable to process depth and is of relatively low detail.

The field of view where our eyes have the greatest amount of detail is quite small: only about 6 degrees of arc. This is where our attention is focused, and everything we see outside of this focus zone has much less detail. You can test this easily by focusing on a word on this page, then trying to read a sentence from higher in the paragraph without shifting your focus from the word. Chances are you can't do it, and if you can you were probably shifting your focus without realizing it. We're able to focus on and read an area of about 5 or so words, but everything around that center-of-both-eyes focus zone is comparatively blurry.

So, what does this mean for VR headsets? Well, the larger your field of view, the more immersed you'll feel in the virtual world. Modern headsets tend to have an FOV of around 100 degrees horizontal and 110 degrees vertical, but it varies by headset. Even though part of your vision is blocked by blackness in the headset, this 100 degree FOV seems to be enough to induce presence and get people to forget they are wearing a headset. More expansive FOVs are desirable to increase immersion, but creating a larger FOV means creating a larger screen, which means an increase in screen weight and computer hardware for rendering.

Foveated Rendering is a technique still being researched that would allow more efficient rendering performance by only drawing what's in your zone of focus with high resolution (i.e. high detail), and using low resolution for the rest of the image. Foveated Rendering requires eye tracking technology (which we'll talk more about later), and may never work effectively, but is an interesting possibility for increasing efficiency without faster computers.

A last note on VR field of view is that it actually changes depending on headset inter-pupillary distance (IPD), which is the distance your eyes are from each other. Many headsets allow you to adjust the IPD to match your own eyes, and changing this setting can increase or decrease your FOV. Adjusting headsets to your personal IPD is important because it will make the lenses in the headset line up correctly for your specific eyes, increasing image sharpness and decreasing eye strain.

Presence

Presence is the feeling of actually being somewhere. It is the visceral feeling of immersion that makes us perceive ourselves as physically experiencing a reality. Look around the room you are in. Take note of something near you. Can you touch it? How do you know what you're seeing is real?

Our bodies have several sensory systems: eyes, ears, touch receptors, taste buds, smell receptors, and more. Our brain takes this sensory information and processes it into a simulated experience. This simulated experience is what we perceive every moment of our lives. We don't ever see a fully objective reality, because the processing of our senses distorts that reality.

For example, look at the following tables. Which one is bigger?:

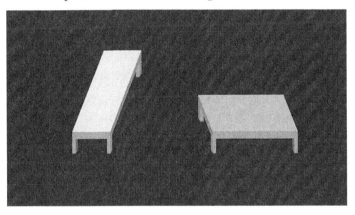

Picture credit Michael Abrash: https://www.oculus.com/blog/vrs-grand-challenge-michael-abrash-on-the-future-of-human-interaction/

It's a trick question, they're actually the same size. No matter how hard you try the table on the left looks longer and thinner than the table on the right, but if you turn the table on the left without altering it, its top lines up perfectly with the table on the right. This illusion is known as the Shepard's Table illusion.

How is this possible? Despite "objective reality" displaying two tables of equal size, our brains are so well trained to pick up on depth cues that when the sensory input comes in, our brains convert the image

BEFORE we perceive it. Our perception of reality can be flawed.

With the right technology, we can fool our brain even further. VR is such a technology. By combining a large field of view with accurate head tracking, a high refresh rate, and 3D stereoscopy, we are able to hijack our senses and trick our brain into believing we are somewhere that we are not. With any of these pieces missing, the experience will fail to induce presence, or offer a diluted presence.

Lack of field of view means your window into the virtual world will be artificially reduced, constantly reminding you that you're looking through a window rather than being present in the virtual world. Lack of accurate head tracking tech means your visuals won't update at the rate and exact amount you move your head, creating a jarring and nauseating disconnect between your motion and that of the virtual world. Lack of a high refresh rate will cause you to see the screen lagging behind your own movements, cause visual artifacts like smear, and cause sickness. Finally, lack of 3D stereoscopy will leave the virtual world feeling noticeably flat, and can cause eye strain issues. When all four components work in tandem we have a working VR headset that achieves presence, something that is available off-the-shelf today.

It is hard to impart how unique VR presence really is. It is the kind of thing that must be experienced first hand to truly understand. If you haven't tried modern VR, I highly encourage you to do so (check out the Hardware chapter for headset recommendations). Intellectual understanding is no substitute for direct personal experience.

Sim Sickness

Sim Sickness, also known as Cybersickness or Visually Induced Motion Sickness, is an unpleasant feeling that can be caused by VR use, as well as by fast paced video games and other types of simulators. Symptoms include nausea, headaches, eye strain, dizziness, and more. The symptoms are temporary and can be relieved by taking a break from VR use.

Modern VR hardware, when running well designed and optimized VR software, is able to avoid sim sickness in the majority of people. Knowing how to avoid causing sim sickness is a vitally important part of VR design and development.

So, why can VR make us feel bad? We don't fully understand it, and it is an active area of research, but we have some theories that seem to make sense and offer actionable design solutions that have proven to work.

Essentially, there are sacs of fluid in our inner ear that help us keep track of motion, head position, and spatial orientation. These sacs and their connecting parts are known as the Vestibular System. The vestibular system does useful things like helping us keep balance and tracking our relative speed.

Sim sickness, it is theorized, occurs when there is a disconnect between what the vestibular system tells us and what our eyes see. As we said earlier, our conscious experience is simulated by our brain based on our sensory input. When a disconnect occurs between what we expect to be feeling and what we actually are feeling, our brain gets disoriented and thinks something is wrong. One of the common beliefs about why this may have developed is as a survival tactic. If you eat a poison mushroom and your vision starts to swim, your body's natural inclination is to expel the toxin.

Motion sickness and sim sickness are closely related. When people get sick in a car, it is because their vestibular system senses them moving, but their visuals don't change inside the car. For this reason, drivers rarely experience motion sickness, while backseat passengers experience it much more often. Next time you're on the road as a passenger, if you suffer from car sickness try to keep your eyes looking outside the car in the direction you are going, rather than inside.

Some people are completely immune to sim sickness and motion sickness, while others are very susceptible. We all exist on a spectrum between the two extremes.

For VR, sim sickness has hardware causes and software causes. First, the hardware:

The frame rate shown by a display can have a large effect on sim sickness. If a display shows 90 fps but then randomly dips down below that number (called "dropping frames"), then most users not immune to sim sickness will feel it. If the default frame rate is too low (a figure that is variable for each person), then that person will feel sim sickness. 60 fps is the bare minimum to avoid this, but many people require higher frame rates for lengthy usage.

If head tracking does not match your movement exactly to within a smaller-than-perceivable range, the visuals of your world will either appear to lag or not move as you expect them to, causing sim sickness. Imagine if when you turned your head, the image didn't change and stayed stuck to your face. Luckily, modern head tracking and display tech are capable of delivering an experience that is comfortable for the majority of people.

On the software side, artificial locomotion (movement) is the number one cause of motion sickness (apart perhaps from dropped frames). If you move around a virtual space with your own two legs in a 1:1

ratio, almost no one will get sick with a Vive or Oculus Rift (90 fps computer-powered headsets). However, if you press a button and your virtual self moves forwards, suddenly you have a problem. Your eyes say you are moving, but your vestibular system says you are stationary. Other movements, such as turning the user's viewpoint, can be even more jarring. Imagine if the world suddenly started spinning around you. This is possible in VR and an unpleasant experience.

Crafting VR experiences that are comfortable for everyone, therefore, relies upon tricks that get around our vestibular system's interference. In the chapter on Software Design we'll explore these tricks in thorough detail. However, the number one consideration is that virtual acceleration, above all else, will cause sim sickness. Vection, the physical sensation of movement seen by the eyes, will cause sim sickness in people to varying degrees and intensities. Linear movement is more comfortable than acceleration, meaning that it is often better to instantly hit top speed than to slowly increase someone's speed.

Because vection and acceleration cause sim sickness, "teleport" has become a popular industry standard that guarantees comfort. When you don't see any motion but just suddenly appear in a new location, there is no vection, and thus no sim sickness.

Of course, for certain types of intense experiences, especially in gaming, users need some vection. Sim sickness tolerance can be built up. Genetics likely play a factor in how susceptible we are, but repeated exposure can increase our tolerance. Astronauts undergo training to be able to handle zero gravity, which often causes nausea, and similarly we can train our brains to handle things like artificial locomotion.

Olfactory (smell) and airflow also play a role in sim sickness. If you're feeling sea-sick it's common to step out from belowdecks to get a breath of fresh air. Ultimately sim sickness is our brain's reaction to stimulus, so it's possible to trick our brains into feeling more comfortable. Even writing this section made me feel mild effects of sim sickness. Our brains are amazing!

Despite the obstacles of sim sickness, the technology and software know-how exist today to avoid it. Although there is still plenty of room for new ideas in the space, we're much further than when I started in 2014. Software design tricks abound for removing or reducing sim sickness, and we'll cover them in detail in the Software Design chapter.

Augmented Reality (AR)

Augmented Reality (AR) is the mixing of 3D computer generated images into the physical world. With AR we still see the physical world around us, but add in 3D (and 2D) images. These added-in 3D images are known colloquially as holograms.

With VR you step into another world, but with AR you bring elements from a digital world into your existing reality. As a simple example, you could be sitting at your desk with an AR hologram of the Mona Lisa hanging on the wall beside you and a small 3D dog sitting on your desk.

Unlike VR, AR doesn't require a headset. Smartphones and tablets are capable of creating an AR window. However, the experience and immersiveness can be markedly improved with a head mounted display (HMD). Long-term, the goal for AR would be a glasses or visor form-factor with a large field of view.

So, what technologies are needed for AR? Like VR, you need accurate positional tracking, high frame rate, and stereoscopic 3D. Additionally, you need a way to display 3D that still allows you to see the physical world, so a simple pixel-based screen probably doesn't work. You would ideally also have a large field of view, but smaller fields of view can still work for certain applications. Since I already covered many of these concepts in the VR section of this chapter, I will stick to AR specific tech here.

Mixed Displays

As of 2020, the main approach for AR HMDs has been to use transparent screens that mix the light of the physical world with the light of the display. Essentially, light from the display and light from the physical world enter an "optical combiner", which overlays the images and redirects the final image to your eye. Take a look at the following image to see the difference between the typical VR and AR display.

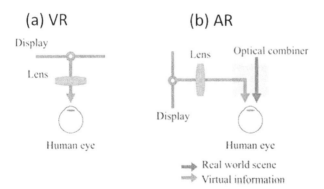

Source: https://virtualrealitypop.com/understanding-waveguide-the-key-technology-for-augmented-reality-near-eye-display-part-i-2b16b61f4bae

Devices such as the Magic Leap One and Hololens 2 use "waveguide" technology to achieve a convincing optical combine. A waveguide is like a fiber optic cable, except used for the visual spectrum of light. Unfortunately, waveguide displays are still fairly limited and it is not clear what type of waveguide system, if any, will be used for large field of view (FOV) AR headsets. So rather than going into excruciating detail about how the displays work, just know that AR displays need to somehow display a combination of the physical and digital world, and that as of early 2020 the FOV created by these devices is noticeably smaller than that of our vision, creating an immersion-breaking window you have to look through to see the holograms.

In the future, and as a completely different approach, we may use AR HMDs that look like VR-headset-like visors, where the outside world is completely blocked off, but high definition cameras on the outside of the headset construct the world as if we were seeing it from our own eyes. There are huge hurdles to making something like this work, including advanced use of machine learning to construct the final image, but it's an intriguing idea.

SLAM (Simultaneous Localization and Mapping)

SLAM is the technology that allows an AR device to know where it is in physical space. You can think of it as a form of estimated triangulation using sensors. It is location tracking that can be used anywhere, rather than in a pre-configured room.

For a mobile AR device to work properly, its SLAM system must overcome four challenges. First, it has to be able to locate itself in an unknown space, so that the device can be used anywhere without pre-setup. Second, it must be able to adjust its positioning knowledge based on a user-controlled camera, meaning from the software's standpoint the camera is completely uncontrolled. Third, the device must update its positional knowledge in real-time (ideally 60 Hz or faster). Fourth, its positional knowledge must stay consistent over time, without drift.

An example of drift is if you were to put a virtual coffee cup on your table, look away, and when you look back the coffee cup is 6 centimeters to the right of where it was previously. In reality, we expect objects to stay where we put them, so drift not only breaks immersion, but can make using AR frustrating. My miniature virtual goat I lovingly placed on my desk is now phasing through the desk when I look back, with only the horns showing. A good SLAM system corrects for drift to keep the virtual world as consistent as the physical one.

To overcome the challenges of real time localization and mapping, AR devices need sensors and an algorithm that processes that sensor data. The trifecta of sensors most commonly used are cameras, a gyroscope, and an accelerometer. Additional sensors such as GPS, light sensors, depth sensors, and more can also be used.

The AR device attempts to build a model of the world it is seeing through the sensors. Each frame captured by the camera / depth-sensor is processed by the computer, and a cloud of interest points is usually formed. These interest points are called keypoints. The keypoints of the image form a "point cloud" that represents the computer's understanding of the physical world. For some devices this point cloud is only made up of keypoints, while for others it forms a dense 3D point cloud. On the next camera frame, the algorithm looks at how the keypoints have changed, and combined with the other sensor data (accelerometer, gyroscope, etc), attempts to triangulate how the AR device has moved between frames. Because the camera data is imperfect, this triangulation is ultimately an estimation, rather than exact.

Over time using an AR device, you generate a map of your surrounding environment. Familiarity with the environment can improve tracking. However, drift can still occur when moving around in an environment then returning to a previous location, because the sensory data estimation doesn't exactly match your movement. SLAM systems use loop closure to correct for this drift, which is a fancy way of saying that the system looks for matching keypoints from previous parts of the map, and when finding enough of them corrects the current state of the map, which should also correct the drift. As we use better sensors and our algorithms improve, SLAM tracking will get even more accurate.

The end result of SLAM is an AR device that can place holograms in any environment, allows the user to move around the environment freely, and keeps the holograms grounded in physical space as if they were part of the physical world. In some cases, the map that SLAM creates can be used for other things such as physics interactions with the world (ex. bouncing a digital ball off your physical desk or placing a virtual Netflix monitor against your wall).

What AR is Not

Google Glass was perhaps the most infamous HMD of recent memory. It allowed users to look in the upper corner of their vision and see a screen, while making people wonder whether they were being filmed. Google Glass was not AR, it was a wearable display with a camera. The image you saw reacted in no way to the environment you were looking at. You just had an extra screen tucked in the corner of your eye, and the ability to record what you were looking at.

Wearable screens with a camera can be useful. For example, surgeons were using them to record their surgeries and send the footage to India to train surgeons there. However, wearable screens are not AR. AR requires the ability to generate holograms: the ability to place images into the physical world so that they seem a part of that world. Some may argue against this strong stance, but I think it's important to explain the unique Presence of AR similarly to that of VR. It's the kind of experience that's straight out of sci-fi, and needs to be tried to be fully comprehended.

Conclusion

There's no doubt that head mounted AR will be a hugely important technology in the future. There's also certain use cases today that offer great value. However, compelling consumer AR will probably not be possible on an HMD until 2025 (although some breakthroughs may allow this to come sooner). Limitations of the hardware and increased cost over VR counterparts means that industry use will take longer than VR, which is ready for mass deployment   now.

Phone and Tablet AR, on the other hand, is widely available and at an affordable price point for many. The downsides of handheld AR compared to an HMD are that one or both hands are occupied with holding the device, you have to consciously aim the device where you want to look, and the field of view is small. That said, there are a number of valuable use cases for handheld AR. For example, Google Translate now allows you to translate words in real time with your camera, and an app called Ink Hunter allows you to see what a tattoo would look like on you. Phone AR has also gained mainstream adoption with things like Snapchat filters that alter your appearance.

Mixed Reality (MR)

Mixed Reality (MR) is the merging of virtual and physical worlds. What exactly does this mean? Well, it encompasses all AR and VR that interacts with both the physical and virtual world. The technical definition of MR is generally seen as a spectrum between AR and VR. The technical definition of MR changes depending on who you ask, and the term is so muddied and vague that its usefulness is diluted.

In many ways, MR can be seen as a precursor to XR, as a way to talk about VR and AR together in one word. It can also be seen as a term that started with good intentions but then was recently co-opted as marketing speak by Microsoft and Magic Leap. Unfortunately, the term seems redundant at this point.

Depending on who you ask, MR could technically exclude any VR headset that doesn't interact with your surroundings at all. Oculus Go, for example, uses an accelerometer and gyroscope to track your head's rotation, so its lack of interacting with the physical world could exclude it from MR. However, perhaps you consider rotation in physical space as interacting with the world, in which case it is MR on the far VR side of the spectrum. You see the dilemma?

Microsoft launched a suite of "Windows Mixed Reality" headsets that use SLAM tracking. The devices are VR headsets that use cameras plus accelerometer and gyroscope to track position in space, so technically they interact with the physical world to keep you in your digital world. But for Neo's sake, it's a VR headset with inside-out tracking (inside-out tracking is a common nomenclature for SLAM that doesn't use external sensors to track device position, i.e. the sensors are all on the device). Muddying the waters further, Magic Leap and Microsoft refer to their AR efforts as mixed reality. From a

PR standpoint, it's likely they were trying to distance their tech from Google Glass, which was incorrectly referred to as AR. Some people would argue against me on this, but I think moving forward it's important to differentiate between AR, which uses fully embodied digital holograms, and wearable screens which just overlay imagery without 3D awareness.

The best use of MR as a term has been to refer to Mixed Reality capture. By using a green screen, well placed cameras, and software wizardry it is possible to combine video of a person using a VR app with the digital world they are seeing. The result is a clearer representation of the person's experience in VR, since you can see their head and hands move in reaction to the virtual environment. First-person footage (i.e. no Mixed Reality capture) can struggle to convey the VR experience due to a smaller field of view than what the user can see and an inability to clearly show any physical movement. Mixed Reality capture can also be done for AR, and green screens are not always necessary.

So, if you hear the term MR, just know that it's referring to AR, VR, or a blend of the two and make sure you understand the specifics of what is being offered.

XR (Extended Reality)

XR has become the spatial computing industry's catch-all term for VR and AR. Spatial Computing (SC) and Immersive Computing (IC) are also commonly used terms for the VR and AR industry. However, the acronyms for those terms (SC and IC) have not taken off. Instead, XR has become the popular leader, since the X could stand for V or A in VR / AR. XR doesn't really stand for anything beyond AR / VR, but could also be called Extended Reality or X-

Reality.

Unfortunately, since VR and AR are such a new field (at least in terms of this new wave) and XR a newly coined term, very few outside of the VR / AR industry know what XR means. Because of this, use of XR for newcomers to the industry can be confusing and offer bad Search Engine Optimization (SEO) to outsiders. Conversely, use of XR can signal insider knowledge to those in the know (although if use of the term continues to grow this will change).

From an industry perspective, I think XR renders MR obsolete (except in the case of MR capture), as it eliminates the obscure definition of MR, and is catchier and more easily equatable to VR / AR. That said, XR is still a new term (it entered the scene around 2016), and so we'll have to wait to see how it develops. We'll probably be using the term AR / VR for a while yet, at least until XR tech is in the majority of homes and part of the mainstream zeitgeist.

Degrees of Freedom

(3DOF vs 6DOF)

XR systems can be divided into two main categories of tracking quality.

3 Degree of Freedom (3DOF) systems only track rotation. The 3 degrees of motion are pitch, yaw, and roll (which correspond to rotational axis). So, if you are wearing a 3DOF headset you can turn your head and the visuals will appear to move correctly, but if you

move your head through space the visuals will not match your movement. Controllers can also be 3DOF, like the Oculus Go remote. You can point with the controller, and in some cases have some approximation of positional change, but really it's just rotational information that is tracked, usually through an accelerometer and gyroscope.

6 Degree of Freedom (6DOF) systems track rotation and position. So, in addition to pitch, yaw, and roll, movement is tracked in the X, Y, and Z axis (i.e. left/right, up/down, forward/back). This means that if you're wearing a 6DOF headset, both your head rotation and movement through space match your change in visuals, offering the same experience as physical reality. Controllers can also be 6DOF, allowing you to feel like your hands are present in the virtual simulation.

These differences are important because of sim sickness, presence, and functional differences. One of the biggest problems with 3DOF headsets is that if a person tries to move their head, their immersion gets broken and they'll experience sim sickness if they are susceptible to it. Additionally, even minute rotation of the head usually involves some positional change, leading to a subtle disconnect between what you see and what your brain expects to see that causes sim sickness. 3DOF controllers can be useful for intuitive laser-pointer-based selection and user interface (UI) interaction, but they act more like an abstract controller than an immersive extension of your hands.

In contrast, 6DOF headsets are capable of keeping users immersed and avoiding vestibular disconnect that results in sim sickness. The sub-millimeter accuracy of the 6DOF controller (and in some cases hand) tracking allows a user to intuitively use their hands in the virtual world.

If 6DOF is so much better, why would someone use a 3DOF headset? Some in the XR industry bemoan that 3DOF is "poisoning the well". New VR users can't easily distinguish between 3DOF and 6DOF, so if their first time using VR is with 3DOF and they get sim sickness, they may feel that VR isn't for them. This is a valid concern, although first-time experiences can be bad no matter what hardware you use if the software is bad. Personally I'm not a fan of 3DOF headsets (we've had cheap 6DOF since 2014!), but there are specific use cases where they actually make sense.

180 and 360 degree stereoscopic or flat video don't benefit from 6DOF. Video has one reference point to be viewed from, and only head rotation can change what is shown regardless of 3DOF or 6DOF hardware. So, if your primary use of VR is physical-world 180 or 360 videos, 3DOF headsets might make sense.

Lightfield capture is a nascent technology that allows you to bring physical world capture to 6DOF. Instead of capturing video from a single reference point, lightfield capture collects data about the light rays in a scene, allowing you to move the viewing angle or depth of focus after capture. Imagine if a director for traditional video could shoot a scene, then later in the editing change the camera angle a little up and to the left. For VR, this means you can use lightfield to capture a scene then move your head in 6DOF while viewing it. This works as long as you keep your head movement within a predetermined cube of space. Lightfield is still in its early days, but the tech is worth keeping an eye on.

Cost is of course another consideration. Since 3DOF headsets will almost certainly always be cheaper than 6DOF ones (less sensors needed), you can save money on hardware with 3DOF. That said, I think the increase in hardware cost for 6DOF is well worth it, especially with devices like the Oculus Quest on the market.

Although technically you might be able to make an AR 3DOF device, none of the leading devices on the market use 3DOF. The entire idea of AR starts to break down if your holograms don't stay put in the world.

There are businesses using 3DOF VR headsets for benefit, and the cheap price point is attractive. However, in the overwhelming number of cases you should use 6DOF headsets, and I expect 3DOF headsets will become an antiquated technology in the medium term future. Sim sickness is a serious concern, and the immersion of 3DOF is severely limiting, resulting in a VR experience that feels half-baked. It says something that Oculus has stopped advertising its 3DOF Oculus Go for Business headset on its website, instead exclusively advertising the 6DOF Oculus Quest.

Standalone vs Tethered

A standalone headset is a VR or AR device that has the computer and sensors all contained in the device. In contrast, a tethered headset connects to an external computer and/or sensors. There is a direct tradeoff between compute power and device mobility.

The standalone / tethered line can be blurred, and is more of a spectrum than mutually exclusive categories. For example, the Magic Leap One connects to a small computer worn on your belt or pocket but has no components separated from the user, making it both standalone and tethered.

Tethered is usually thought of as a cable connecting the XR headset to an external computer (and in some cases sensors). However, some technologies allow wireless transmission of rendering from a computer to a headset. Is tethered still an appropriate word for this? I believe so, because as long as the headset relies on an external computer, it is tethered to that device.

Wireless remote rendering may someday become the norm for XR as we seek to lighten the weight of HMDs. We're already starting to see game streaming services such as Nvidia Geforce Now and Google Stadia, which allow the playing of high performance video games on low performance computer hardware. Admittedly these services are in their infancy and suffer drawbacks that make them as yet inappropriate for XR. However, 5G wireless tech and further developments in processing / information transfer speed could improve the situation.

For now, Standalone and Tethered headsets have trade offs you'll need to consider for your specific use case. We'll explore which headset to use in more detail in the Hardware chapter.

CHAPTER 2:
ADVANTAGES OF
VR / AR

What is it about VR and AR that make them such useful tools for businesses? When affordable computers came to the business world, the game was forever changed. Suddenly you could automate your accounting workflow through software like spreadsheets. What took hours to copy or calculate by hand could be done near-instantly on a computer, resulting in huge productivity gains. Word processing, powerpoint, and more use cases evolved as ways to utilize the unique properties of computers for efficiency gains.

We are at a similar point with XR. VR and AR tech is now cost effective for many businesses. But what advantages do these technologies actually give us? Can't we just stick with our existing computers, rather than paying for new hardware and software? In this chapter we'll explore the myriad ways in which VR and AR provide unique value. In the medium term (5-15 years), XR will be a supplement to flat screen computers rather than a replacement. XR is not useful by default and can actually be worse in some instances, so my hope is that this chapter will equip you with the knowledge to utilize XR to its highest potential.

VR Superpowers

I liked Oculus's characterization of VR's advantages as superpowers, since the tech can truly make you feel like a superhero. For each of the superpowers listed here I'll explain it in detail, give examples, judge its level of value, and evaluate how unique it is to VR. Then we'll do the same for the AR superpowers.

Muscle Memory

Remember at the start of the book when I talked about working memory and chunking? As a quick review, because we have a limited amount we can focus on at one time, we build ways of grouping information together to take up less working memory. One of the ways we can increase our available working memory is by practicing tasks until they become automatic. For example, when we've learned how to drive we no longer have to consciously focus on every aspect of driving. If you've ever started daydreaming while on the road and suddenly found yourself at your destination, you'll know what I'm talking about. Although this can be dangerous because it slows our reaction time to unexpected events, the mere fact that it can happen is amazing, and highlights the value of muscle memory.

Walking is another great example of muscle memory freeing up cognitive load. When you walk somewhere, are you unable to do other cognitive tasks because you are focusing on moving your feet and staying upright? Probably not. However, once upon a time we actually had to learn to walk, and doing so took our full attention. The muscle memory is so ingrained later in life that it provides barely any distraction to our thinking.

VR is an amazing tool for training muscle memory, especially when it comes to procedural knowledge. With VR you can actually do the work you would be doing almost 1:1, something that flat screen computers simply can't achieve. For example, if you need to train for a complicated surgery, you can jump into a simulation of the operating room you'll be using and practice the surgery repeatedly by using your hands and the tools available. The micro-movements of the tools will still need to be practiced separately, but the knowledge of "ok first I need to make an incision with the scalpel here, then I need to grab the brace and place it here" can be automated into muscle memory. Doing so allows the surgeon to focus on monitoring the patient and micro movements when conducting the surgery.

It's also worth mentioning that with specialized hardware, the training can become almost exactly 1:1. For example, pilots have been using simulation training for about a hundred years via simulators that mimic aircraft movement and their controls setup. Tasks like controlling an excavator can be trained with VR using either a virtual or physical control system that matches.

The important advantage that VR offers over flat computers in regard to muscle memory is that it removes the abstraction of the control input. You simply do the task you're training for as if you're doing it in the physical world, building robust muscle memory. In contrast, doing the same type of training through a computer requires you to click with a mouse or your finger while looking at a 2D representation of your workplace. That extra layer of abstraction increases cognitive load. This in turn decreases the rate at which you learn and the transferability of that learning into muscle memory.

Unlimited Repetition

Software allows you to reset to any point the designer has implemented. For example, if you want to practice the same task, such as replacing the wheel on a car, you can do so repeatedly without the tiring physical exertion of doing the task. As we talked about in the previous section, practice is important for building muscle memory, so the ability to practice a given task as many times as we want is extremely valuable. This is an advantage of all software-based training, not just VR, but due to the muscle memory implications of VR training, VR can become an alternative to methods previously reserved for "practical experience".

For example, if training someone to paint a house, you'd typically bring them to a job site and train them on the job (hopefully offering your customer a discount). You, as the painting manager, need to physically spend a lot of time with your new painter making sure they learn to paint the house correctly, and there is still some risk of mistakes being made that either result in time-expensive cleanup, wasted paint, or an unhappy customer. Some people may use software or videos that train things like safety and procedures for painting, but these forms of learning are not very effective and on-site training is a necessity.

In contrast, imagine that you could give your new painter-hire a VR app that trained them to paint a house. The painter could essentially get hours of experience painting houses before ever stepping foot on the job site. Additionally, this training wouldn't come at any expense to your time as a manager, paint cost, or risk to the customer. You could even include evaluation metrics to ensure the painter was ready to work on a real job site. Sure, you'd probably still want to be there for their first job, but I think you'd find that with the right paint training software you'd soon find yourself unneeded there.

Another example is surgery training, which traditionally uses cadavers (i.e. dead bodies). Cadavers are limited in supply, and once you use one you can't really use it again. With VR, you can replace the cadaver for an unlimited number of practice sessions, at no additional cost other than your own time. Because of this, it's no surprise that surgeons are one of the longest standing and quickest adopting users of VR.

These are just a few examples, but I hope it's clear that Unlimited Repetition combined with the unique Muscle Memory aspects of VR offer a huge advantage in learning efficiency, performance, and cost savings.

High Stakes with No Risk

VR is a great way to train for something where mistakes are dangerous or costly. For example, if you work on an oil rig, mistakes are both dangerous and costly. You wouldn't trust a complete newbie to learn on a multi-million dollar oil rig, where mistakes could cause an environmentally disastrous oil spill and explosion of your expensive equipment. You would conduct extensive training before that worker ever set foot on the rig, and would need to supervise that new worker for an extended period of time once on the job site.

Also, how do you train someone for what to do if things go wrong? You're not going to cause a hardware malfunction that could cause damage just for the point of training, and too many "fire drills" on the actual site can have the unintended consequence of making people less likely to take emergency situations seriously.

VR training allows you to simulate the work on an oil rig almost exactly, and allows you to repeatedly train for rare and potentially dangerous situations. Additionally, failure is an important part of learning. By allowing the new trainee to fail at their task during a training scenario, they are able to learn from their mistakes and repeat the task until it's in their muscle memory. Not only is there cost savings in terms of trainer time and facility usage, but the trainee gains mastery at their job without putting anyone at risk.

This high stakes no risk principle can be applied across many industries. For example, train high voltage power line repair workers with a VR sim, so that a rookie mistake doesn't mean ZAP you're dead. The worker can gain a visual feel for how far away they are from a power line, and get comfortable with the tasks they'll have to do, with the instant feedback that they're making mistakes without the feedback being physically dangerous.

No surprise, surgery training takes advantage of this by allowing a surgeon to perform a new surgery multiple times without risking harm to a patient. The scary thing is, before VR surgeons trained by watching other surgeons perform a surgery or via limited hands-on training, and so little muscle memory was involved! A rare operation might be tried for the first time on a patient without mastery of the technique!

Flat computer simulations can also allow failure in a high risk environment without the risk. However, there is a very different quality to doing the work as you actually would, rather than doing it abstractly on a flat interface (i.e. muscle memory and efficiency of learning is increased for VR). For high risk training, both safety wise and monetarily, VR training will provide a large amount of benefit.

3D Efficiencies

For any form of 3D work, whether it's designing a car or creating a game character, there are significant efficiency gains to working directly in 3D.

For work where you are designing physical objects for the real world, VR allows you to feel what the product would actually look like in reality, since you are able to mimic the sense of scale for the object. Car designers can actually sit inside their car design and make adjustments on the fly. With traditional flat screen workflows, you have to guess at scale using measurements, and don't have a true understanding of your product until you manufacture test versions. With VR, you can instantly experience your end product visually with the correct scale, without any manufacturing required. For example, a team at Ford using the app Gravity Sketch for its car designs claims that a process that used to take them months now only takes 20 hours.

Even for 3D art that is going to remain digital, VR allows quick and intuitive repositioning of your head to see a model from different angles, rather than the traditional flat screen workflow of moving an abstract camera view. If you want to rotate your model with VR, you can do so naturally with your hands rather than rotating via abstract commands.

These two advantages combine to make 3D modelling a more intuitive, and thus easier to learn process. Additionally, some experienced 3D artists find the workflow more efficient than their flat screen counterpart. The tools to allow modelling and design in VR are still evolving, but they appear promising. Also, it may seem obvious, but the best way to make VR / AR models seems to be doing it in VR, since the scale matching and experience of the end user match that of the artist.

Flat screens simply can't compete with XR when it comes to intuitively understanding a 3D model.

Telepresence (Remote Realtime Embodied Collaboration)

VR creates presence, the feeling of actually being someplace. With modern VR headsets, this presence can combine with virtual embodiment, the feeling of having control of your body in a virtual setting. Presence and virtual embodiment overlap, but the primary difference is that virtual embodiment specifically refers to feeling like you can control a virtual hand or move a virtual body like it is yours (your body and the virtual body are one). Presence is the overall feeling that results from visual immersion, virtual embodiment, and other sensory immersion (such as 3D spatialized sound).

Telepresence is any technology that allows a person to feel like they are somewhere else, or have the appearance of being somewhere else, in a social context. Video conferencing such as Skype is a form of telepresence, since it lets people see each other remotely, allowing important communication tools such as body language.

VR allows powerful telepresence. Not only can you use important body language such as hand gestures, but the communication and collaboration can be interactive, rather than passive like video. For example, car designers use the VR app Gravity Sketch to work on their designs simultaneously. They can point to a feature of the car, such as the steering wheel, talk about possible changes, then make alterations to the wheel immediately in real time.

"I think the wheel needs to be a bit bigger."
"(Adjusts the wheel size) How about this?"
"Even bigger."
"Now?"
"Perfect"

Not only can this high-bandwidth communication be interactive, but it can be conducted remotely. A designer in Norway can collaborate with a designer in Canada. Oculus likes to tout the message "Defy Distance" because VR allows us to work and socialize with a fidelity approaching that of the physical-world.

Another example of the usefulness of telepresence is that of remote guided instruction. If showing someone how to repair a piece of machinery remotely, pointing to relevant pieces is more helpful than purely explaining what to do with words.

Whether a team is remote or in person, VR collaboration offers advantages. However, the currently available technology still has some shortcomings, meaning it won't replace in-person work completely. Designing around these shortcomings will be important for the short to medium term.

For example, communication latency (i.e. delay) can cause remote collaboration to be less smooth. If you've ever spoken to someone on video chat and they started talking over you, then you both stopped, you've probably experienced communication latency. This situation happens in physical-world conversations too, but it's more prevalent in online communication since there can be a delay of hundreds of milliseconds before your words and actions reach that of the person you are talking to.

Network speeds and bandwidth have gotten a lot better over the last several years, bringing communication latency over the internet down to a level where it's possible to hold a conversation with anyone across the globe. However, because of physical limits to the speed of light and thus communication, a person in Tokyo, Japan and New York, USA will still experience about 209 milliseconds of latency. Additionally, increased distance comes with increased packet loss, meaning more bits of data can get lost in transit.

This all means that people on separate sides of the world can collaborate remotely, but with a slightly lower quality of experience. For this reason, geography still plays some role in how you set up your remote teams (along with time zone differences). However, even a quarter of a second of latency (250 milliseconds) can be tolerable for many applications, and closer geographies offer latency below what can be noticed.

Another downside of VR communication compared to in-person or video is that as of right now, faces are not tracked. This means you can communicate with your voice, head and hand movements, and gestures (such as pointing, etc) but not with eye cues or facial expressions.

Although this is not ideal, the communication bandwidth that VR provides beats video for anything where 3D position in an environment matters. You can't point to a specific object in a shared space with video. Even in its current form VR communication is rich enough for effective communication, shown through a study of whether VR Pictionairy players suffered performance drops compared to in-person Pictionairy (they didn't).

Future VR headsets will likely support facial and eye tracking, alleviating this weakness.

Possible Impossible Scenarios

VR simulations allow training scenarios that would otherwise be impossible or very impractical. For example, if you want a plane pilot to get practice dealing with an engine explosion, it's impractical, expensive, and dangerous to do that in physical reality. In a VR sim, you can practice that scenario repeatedly.

Memorizing steps to do in the case of an engine failure is relatively ineffective since it doesn't give you the practical feel. A flat screen simulation is more helpful, but the 2D to 3D translation makes learning this way less transferable. VR puts the pilot in a scenario as close to reality as possible, so that if an engine explodes they are prepared to recognize the problem, and do what they can to safely land the plane.

What if you wanted to train a hundred astronauts for flight to Mars? Use of the spacecraft for training would be limited, and any number of things could go wrong on the way that the crew may have to remedy. Although you could possibly build an entire simulation spacecraft and run through estimated simulations on it, VR offers a cheaper and more flexible solution. In many cases where physical simulation could be used, VR offers cost savings that makes training of certain scenarios possible that would otherwise be out of budget or impractical.

Knowledge Confidence

Workers like to feel empowered. It can be scary trying something new. Failure at a given task could result in injury, unhappy customers, reprimand, or firing. We want to provide our employees with training that leaves them confident that they know what to do.

With non-VR learning methods, there is often some level of anxiety trying a new task "live" in the workplace (except jobs conducted solely on a computer). This is because the worker has never done the task before, they've only learned about how to do the job. With VR, you do the work as you would do it in the workplace, and this 1:1 comparison builds worker confidence in their knowledge.

For example, surgeons must take examinations where they perform mock surgeries. A study found that surgeons who trained with VR compared to traditional methods completed the procedure in far less time, and had to ask the supervising surgeon for much less guidance.

Increased Engagement

Engagement is a term used to describe someone who is attentive on something and not bored. Engagement is important for learning because it increases retention and the desire to continue learning. For example, someone learning about how to cook fried chicken at KFC may find a video of the steps fairly boring. KFC decided to create a VR escape room in which you had to cook the chicken to escape from a horror-like room. You can imagine that such a scenario would seem more interesting.

However, this experiment kind of missed the point, and failed to take into account cognitive science research from the past two decades. Engagement can be increased through the addition of frills, such as creepy music and cool visuals, but ultimately it is what we put our attention on that we remember. Engaging elements can actually distract away from the things we want people to learn. If you try to learn chicken cooking, but a lot of your time is spent listening to a music box, you'll remember the music box, not how to cook chicken.

Therefore, it's important to avoid engaging elements that are overly distracting from your focused goal. Luckily, it turns out that mastery and active learning are engaging in their own right! The problem with videos, lectures, and other passive learning is that they are passive! Just by doing something, you're more engaged.

How engaged someone is in a task depends on their skill level and the difficulty of the task at hand. When a task is too easy, we get bored. When it is too hard, we get frustrated. In the middle we have tasks that engage our minds in ways that are rewarding (we generate happiness neurochemicals when successfully completing tasks).

Therefore, a better training VR app for KFC would be to place users into a replica kitchen, have them learn the steps of making chicken, then challenge them to cook multiple batches of the chicken under a time restraint, allowing things like burned or improperly prepared chicken, but having that give immediate negative feedback in the form of subtracting your score. Gamification has been studied a lot in the past two decades, and although there is still much to learn about how game elements can improve learning, increased engagement is a strong one.

So, VR can offer increased engagement over traditional media, even flat screen games, given the right circumstances. The tech is still so new that it creates engagement in new users by default, but as it becomes common in the workplace the novelty will wear off. Ensuring VR remains engaging requires utilizing the powers the medium has to offer (such as presence, simulation, and interactivity).

Note: There are some studies that show VR as more engaging than traditional media in apples-to-apples comparisons, but there could be a number of confounding factors.

Distraction Reduction

With a VR headset on you are mostly shut off from the outside world. There is reduced social distraction because you can't see the people around you, and the sound of the physical world may be muffled by the sound of the app you are running. Looking at your phone or computer monitor is difficult. The friction of having to put the headset on or off means that once you are in VR, you're going to avoid taking the headset off until you've finished your task or need a break.

Additionally, as of right now the VR operating systems are limited in terms of notifications and parallel processing. You can browse the web or use social media when you want to, but if you are in an app you can't quickly shift over to another app then back to the app you were in at the state you were in. Some systems, such as the Oculus Rift or Quest, allow users to pull up a system overlay in any app, but this overlay is restricted to web browsing and a select number of other functions.

So, for enterprise use cases where your user isn't connected to the internet, or is constrained to specific apps, VR offers a reduction in distractions compared to other methods. People using a monitor to watch a video can pull out their phones, and people using flatscreen computers can easily tab over to Facebook, Youtube, or a video game without quitting the app they're supposed to be using.

As VR adoption increases and the ecosystem evolves, VR will lose some of this distraction reduction. If all your coworkers and friends are also in VR, they can join you virtually. Notifications will increase and get further integrated into the platform, and VR operating systems will gain the ability to multitask. Some hardware improvements such as camera pass-through visuals might get good enough to mimic our eyes seeing the world, allowing us to switch back and forth between VR and the physical world without taking the headset off.

So, VR currently offers some distraction reduction but don't count on that lasting in the long term.

Varied Perspectives

VR has a unique capacity for empathy building. You can step into the life of someone else, living that life from an immersive first person perspective.

Two studies conducted by Stanford University put VR's empathy ability to the test. Unlike some prior studies which looked at short-term effects with small sample sizes, these studies looked at more than 560 people over a 2 month period. Participants were shown a

VR simulation called "Becoming Homeless", a 2D version of the sim, or a written narrative about homelessness.

As the name implies, "Becoming Homeless" put participants in an interactive scenario that showed what it could be like to become homeless. For those who did the VR sim, 85% later signed a petition for affordable housing, compared to 66% for the 2D version and 63% for the written narrative.

As our world becomes more globally connected, and the gap between our rich and poor grows, VR can help us empathize and connect more effectively than other forms of media.

Increased Metrics

In our data-hungry age, VR offers more precise tracking of human intention and behavior than ever before possible. This potential for behavioral tracking is perhaps the most hotly debated topic within the XR industry, as it has significant privacy and ethics implications.

Before we get into ethics, let's consider what exactly VR allows you to track. With current hardware you can track head and hand movement and rotation. Some equipment supports partial or full finger tracking. The capacity also exists for voice recording and button-press tracking. All of this data can be tied to specific contexts within the VR simulation that is running.

For example, if a user is buying something through a VR store, how long do they look at an item before they buy it? If learning how to fix a car engine, how long do they spend in the guided repair section versus doing time trial practice?

Headsets in the future will likely include eye and facial tracking. Eye tracking is already available in specialized headsets, and facial tracking could be added to a headset if you spent a lot of money. The affordability of these two technologies will increase over time, and I expect that they'll both be included in the default headset within 10 years (and probably sooner).

Just because these data sources can be tracked, should they be? What are the implications of increased tracking input?

Well, first let's consider that tracking on flat devices allows things like mouse or touch movement tracking, as well as context such as how long you spend on a given page, or where you are when you use your device. Even with those limited inputs, data like how you move your mouse and browse a web page can be used to identify you. Use a web page that employs tracking one time, and even if you use a VPN (Virtual Private Network) and Tor to anonymize yourself, a return visit to the web page may still mark you as the original individual.

VR tracking offers a lot more data than mouse movement, and machine learning algorithms are getting more advanced. They are able to see patterns where they never could before. Because of this, it's likely that even with your username anonymized, VR tracking data could be correlated to your unique identity. No matter where you go online in VR, your movement-behavior profile could be tracked. Over time it may become impossible to be anonymous on apps that utilize this kind of tracking.

So, privacy could be threatened by VR. An interesting example of the technology-privacy debate that I'd consider both nefarious and potentially useful is the testing of brainwave-monitoring headbands for tracking students' attention in classrooms. Although not specifically VR, what should we think about students having their brains tracked? VR offers tracking not unlike brainwave tracking, and the tech could be incorporated into future VR headsets.

The arguments for it are that it allows a teacher or school feedback about the health of their students, as well as feedback on the effectiveness of certain lessons. Some arguments against it are that it encourages students to game the devices (i.e. concentrate on anything, not necessarily the lesson, just to not appear lazy) and it acts as an invasion of privacy that could give students anxiety.

Is student attention-tracking ethical? Is it effective at increasing the rate of learning? Neither of these questions has been fully answered. My gut reaction is that it's a dystopian Orwellian nightmare, but I also recognize that if the tech is used in a holistic way, it could offer valuable feedback to the learning loop.

I think most ethics debates orbit around the way things are implemented. Is it ethical to kill a cow slowly with stab wounds? No. Is it ethical to kill it quickly for the purpose of meat? Most of society says yes, but there are still some who say no. Similarly, I think mandatory brain tracking where you were reprimanded for inattention would be terrible. If you used the technology sparingly to test specific lessons to see how effective they were, and the students agreed to it, I think it could be valuable. Technology is a double edged sword.

How can the increased metrics of VR be used ethically? There is much work of discovery and debate to figure out the answer to that question. However, here are my early suggestions:

First, it is important that users know what is being tracked. Hiding this info in a Terms of Service agreement is almost criminal. If a service needs to use VR metrics, there should be a plain non-legalese description of what info is being tracked.

Second, colluding or selling this data across services is better avoided, since it violates peoples' privacy and exposes their data to increased chance of breach.

Third, the use of the data should be for holistic purposes, not predatory ones. For example, if you are creating a training simulation for surgeons, the metrics from VR could allow you to improve the simulation, and thus improve the skill of the surgeons who are trained, which is a great outcome. In contrast, using the data to track when someone is probably experiencing financial trouble so that you can then offer them high interest loans is borderline evil.

For psychology experiments, VR allows an increased access to data for the study. Since the whole point of the study is to use science to figure out more about ourselves and the world, the ethics of this application are as ethical as the designed study.

Hopefully we can implement the powerful data collection capabilities of VR for improved productivity without hurting privacy and autonomy.

Cost Savings

Although cost savings dip into the other VR superpowers we have talked about, I think examining them explicitly is important. In the right situations VR can save money, a benefit businesses can enjoy even without taking into account the other harder-to-track advantages.

One of the ways VR can save on cost is by reducing the need for business travel. If the work you need to do with someone is best done in VR, there isn't much reason to fly out to be in the same physical location. For example, architects can walk their clients through new iterations of their building designs, getting instant feedback, without needing to see the client in person. This cost saving can apply to a wide range of VR uses, including allowing a personal instructor to teach from the comfort of their own home. These cost savings can be significant, since travel is costly in terms of dollars, time, and energy.

The automation of VR headsets allows cost savings in terms of people hours as well. For example, an in-person instructor has to be paid for each hour of teaching. If you are able to instead create VR instruction software that handles the teaching, you can re-use the software without having to waste the instructors time teaching the same concept repeatedly. This isn't necessarily a bad thing for instructors, since a single instructor can now deploy their teaching at a scale that would be impossible if they had to teach every person by being there physically. Additionally, the teaching can be obtained on demand during times that are individually convenient and efficient, instead of at a pre-set time.

The performance increases of VR software also act as a financial benefit. Better-trained workers are less likely to make mistakes that cost the company money. In dangerous occupations, injury or death can be very expensive to a company, so reducing the number of accidents is very valuable (both financially, and in terms of the priceless cost of human life). Even for non-dangerous occupations mistakes are still expensive. For example, an inspector who misses water damage at a home may lose a future customer, get sued, or have to spend extra resources fixing their mistake.

Performance increases can also translate into higher efficiency, both in the speed of learning and the task itself. If a worker would normally take 20 hours of training to be ready for work, but instead takes 10, you're saving 10 x their hourly rate per worker that you train. In the example of Ford using VR for design collaboration, the efficiency gains of the software save their team hundreds of hours of worker time per design, which will translate to massive savings in the cost to develop new car designs.

These are just some of the ways VR can save businesses money, but I hope it has you thinking about how VR can save money in your own industry. Also, keep in mind that VR has other benefits that are more difficult to measure (such as more engaged employees).

AR Superpowers

Augmented Reality shares many of the superpowers of Virtual Reality, as well as having a few unique ones. For this section I'll talk about how each of the superpowers applies to AR (or whether it doesn't), as well as discuss the unique AR superpowers.

Muscle Memory

AR allows the building of muscle memory like VR, with the added benefit that you can more easily use the exact hardware and tools of your job. In VR you are approximating the muscle memory, focusing more on procedure than the fine motor control. With AR, you can perform the exact action on the machine you want to use with instructional overlay.

For example, if learning to fix a sink you can practice turning an actual wrench while the AR headset marks what direction the wrench should turn, and when procedurally you should turn it (ex. now that you've turned off the water pressure, loosen the bolt). Of note, however, is the fact that tracking technology for AR is still less reliable than VR. Writing software that tracks a random object like a wrench and has that wrench interact with a virtual component is a difficult engineering challenge, and not yet available off the shelf.

Over time the hardware and software will improve to be more environmentally aware, allowing easier interaction between virtual and physical elements, but as of now the technology is still new and a bit janky. For example, AR can detect floor planes and sometimes wall planes, as well as generate an approximate 3D point cloud of the real-world environmental objects, but these systems still suffer from some drift and frequent occasional errors (i.e. errors that happen relatively rarely, but frequently enough that you'll notice them happen).

Another consideration is whether the task you are training muscle memory for requires the physical world. For example, if you need to train in an environment that isn't easily available to you, VR makes more sense, as your AR simulation will essentially be trying to be a VR simulation, but with the added distraction of real world visuals.

Unlimited Repetition

The software component of AR means that you can repeat whatever you are training as many times as you want, just like with VR. If the AR training is mixed with components in the physical world, however, you'll need to consider what is required to reset those components, since unlike the software they can't just be "restarted". For example, if you use AR to learn how to bake a cake while using the physical ingredients, you'll need to get more ingredients to try again since all the ingredients have been physically turned into a cake with no way back.

High Stakes with No (or Lower) Risk

With AR you can still train in a no-risk environment like with VR, however, you can also take AR into a high-stakes environment to potentially reduce risk, depending on the use case. For example, if conducting heart surgery you may wear an AR device that has your notes and procedural knowledge available to assist you, reducing the chance of deadly mistakes.

Lockheed Martin used AR overlays to assist with the tightening of components on spacecraft. Rather than working from a 2D sheet of paper and trying to translate that to the spacecraft, they could directly mark what parts needed to be tightened in which direction, and kept track of the parts that had been completed. Not only was this an efficiency gain, but it made mistakes less likely (and mistakes on a spacecraft could have explosive consequences).

3D Efficiencies

AR shares the 3D efficiency benefits of VR, with the added benefit that you can directly compare 3D digital images to images in the real world. For example, a safety inspector can be looking at a 3D model of a machine part while looking at the actual machine, seeing if the part looks how it should.

3D modeling tools for AR are less developed, and the hardware mostly uses mobile processors, which are hard to do computationally demanding tasks like modeling on. Control inputs for current AR devices are also limited compared to VR, which can use 6DOF controllers for precise control.

Telepresence

The potential for medium to long term AR telepresence is having a conversation with someone remotely as if they were physically in your room. Unfortunately, we aren't quite there yet (at least without very expensive custom hardware).

When working with someone remotely, the presence of AR telepresence is reduced from that of VR (smaller field of view, hologram drift, limited tracking on hands). If working in the same physical space, however, AR offers some advantages such as being able to see the world and each other in addition to the holograms.

Some forms of AR telepresence are very useful. For example, the company Prince Castle uses AR to walk fast-food workers through machine repairs. Rather than having to send a repairman on-site, they can connect the repairman to a local worker and guide them through the repair using AR.

Possible Impossible Scenarios

Creating scenarios that would normally be impossible or impractical is also a strength of AR, but more limited than that of VR since you still have to deal with the physical world around you.

Knowledge Confidence

With AR you can bring increased knowledge confidence directly into the work you are doing, since you can see the physical world in addition to the digital imagery. The Lockheed Martin example from earlier (seeing where to tighten components) is a great example of this. AR can train people to feel more confident about what they know (as with VR), but can also act as an at-work cheat sheet for knowledge and procedures. Compare the new grocery store employee who has to memorize the locations of all items vs one who can quickly search the location of an item with instructions of how to get to the item from where they currently are.

Increased Engagement

AR can increase engagement like VR, with the added benefit that it is available on smartphones and tablets (which many people already have access to). Digital advertising agencies are seeing increased engagement of 30% and 11x the "dwell time" on their smartphone AR ads compared to non-AR ads.

Distraction Reduction

Since AR interfaces with the physical world, distractions like your phone and colleagues are still easily accessible. Because of this, AR does not benefit from distraction reduction like VR.

Varied Perspectives

AR is somewhat capable of putting us in another person's shoes, but projects looking to focus on this aspect of XR would be better off using VR (at least with 2020 hardware). AR can't really change the color of your own skin, or effectively change the entire environment around you.

The empathy potential of AR shines in its ability to interface with the physical world. For example, an AR app that recognizes facial expressions on people around you and labels them may be useful for teaching people with social disorders how to recognize other peoples' emotions. I'm not saying we should do this, I'm only bringing it up as an example of how AR can overlay information and holograms not only onto objects but also the people around you.

If you think Snapchat filters are interesting, wait until they're overlaid on peoples' physical faces as you walk around.

Increased Metrics

All the same VR data such as head and hands movement can be tracked via AR.

AR is potentially an even greater privacy concern since AR cameras can include capture of the places and faces around you. Technically a hacked VR headset could do this (the cameras on the outside of the headset could capture images), but for AR this is practically a feature. AR can be used in the world, so the context that is being captured can be more personal. Imagine if you had an AR app that tracked not only your GPS location but your exact location sub-millimeter as you went about your life. You'd open your dashboard and see how long you spent in any room and the amount of time you talked to each person in your life.

For better or worse that information is there, so it's a matter of ethics, policy, and software engineering that determines whether the data is processed and used.

Hyper Competence

Unlike VR, AR can layer information onto our physical world. As pointed out earlier, this means that you can use an AR device while working with the physical world. Instead of memorizing steps or constantly referencing a guide, you can essentially use AR to cheat on workday tasks. For example, if constructing a building, the AR simulation can show you where you need to place beams of wood, then where those beams need to be nailed together.

IoT (Internet of Things) Telekinesis

Since AR devices are usually mobile and work with the environment around you, they could be useful for using IoT devices (i.e. devices that connect to the internet and can be controlled with software). Need to open your door's smart-lock? Instead of pulling out your phone to do it, you can be wearing an AR device already and just open the door by opening its AR app (or a voice / gesture command).

Honestly I'm not convinced about this use case until AR becomes something comfortable to wear throughout the day, which as of 2020 it is not.

Conclusion

VR and AR offer numerous advantages for business. By combining the knowledge from this chapter and the rest of the book, I hope to help you narrow in on which XR tech can help improve your enterprise, and how to make the most of the technology.

CHAPTER 3:
CASE STUDIES

Now that you have the foundations of what VR / AR are and how to use them, I'd like to give you a smattering of examples from within the industry. There are hundreds of companies already using XR to improve how we work, far more use cases than I could cover in this book. It's also possible that some of the companies presented here may cease to exist within a few years, either bought up, outcompeted, or failing to achieve market success.

That said, I think providing a look at how companies are using VR and AR right now will help you see how the concepts in the earlier part of this book can be put into practice. Rather than trying to start from scratch, you can enter the XR space by jumping off the shoulders of those who came before.

Remember, if a certain case study doesn't seem relevant or you get bored by parts of this chapter, I encourage you to skip ahead to parts that you may find engaging. That said, I'll try to make these examples interesting!

Strivr

Strivr is one of the best known VR training companies. They operate at scale (thousands of headsets) for a plethora of companies.

Sports Training

Strivr got their start working with the National Football League (NFL) to train quarterbacks. By capturing 360 degree video of plays being made on the field, quarterbacks could practice recognizing opponents plays and calling their own plays in response. They could also practice looking for teammates open to passes.

In comparison, the old method of learning new plays and preparing for opponents (often in the form of "quarterback meetings") was to meet with your coach and use X's and O's drawn on a whiteboard. Switching this process to VR allowed the quarterbacks to learn and practice play information directly in the environment where they'd use it, rather than having to transfer 2D knowledge on a board to 3D knowledge on the field. This superpower of VR provided a large benefit in learning speed and retention (as well as confidence). On top of this, the training could be conducted at the quarterback's and coach's own leisure and didn't require the whole team to run drills repeatedly, saving the rest of the team's time and the quarterback's physical energy.

Because they are using VR video exclusively, Strivr has been using 3DOF standalone in the form of the Oculus Go. They claim that for many of their customers, exact accuracy is very important, and so video is their preferred solution. In VR training sessions, the coach often goes through the VR video with the player to provide direct feedback and draw the quarterback's attention to certain things. Strivr can also add virtual coaching and interactivity in the form of questions overlaid on a VR video, receiving immediate feedback of whether you made the right choice.

Strivr's early success expanded, and they now work with a number of NFL and NCAA (the college football league) teams. The Clemson Tigers, their heaviest user in the NCAA, won the national championship in 2019. They've expanded their sports offerings beyond football to basketball and skiing.

From the data they've collected so far, it's clear that VR sports training can provide a competitive advantage in the right context.

Retail Training

It made headlines in 2018 when Walmart announced they'd be putting 17,000 Oculus Go's in the hands of their employees for training. Strivr's work with Walmart showed that VR could be deployed at scale in large enterprises for immediate benefit.

Strivr's training for Walmart has many modules covering topics from checking people out, to empathy training (seeing problematic customers from their point of view), to Black Friday simulations and more. The modules feature 360 video interspersed with quiz questions. It has completely changed the way Walmart trains its employees.

The results speak for themselves. Compared to Walmart's prior training methods, VR achieved 10-15% better knowledge retention and 30% higher employee satisfaction. VR also offers another benefit, namely that it can be used on-demand. Compared to their prior method of teaching employees about "pickup towers", which took 8 hours and involved a physical expert coming to a store for a training day, the VR training was able to teach the same thing in only 15 minutes. Having someone operate a new machine with instant feedback in VR allows them to learn at their own pace and in the same environment they'll be operating in, rather than a classroom lecturer and take-home video which is more passive and less personalized.

Strivr also worked with Verizon to create a safety VR training on how to respond to robberies. It's fairly common for Verizon stores to experience snatch-and-grab or armed robbery since they house a large number of lightweight but expensive electronics. The VR training allowed employees to feel the heart-pounding scenario by placing them in it (safely), and having them make decisions that affected the outcome. It raised the heart rates of many trainees; a stranger speaking threateningly with a gun in VR still seems like they're there to your brain. After a successful pilot, Verizon and Strivr are now deploying this and other VR training modules to 1,600 Verizon stores. Like Walmart, they're adding a number of other modules such as customer service interaction training.

Technicians

Working with the airline JetBlue, Strivr developed training modules for pre-flight safety inspections. Trainees could explore different areas of the aircraft (inside and outside) and identify issues on a timed practice test. This was useful because it allowed new employees to get comfortable with the feeling of being out on the tarmac and navigating the plane, without having to take time on an actual plane (which is costly and limited).

By providing this VR training, they could reduce mistakes that resulted in large costs (such as accidentally deploying the escape slides, which could cost as much as $50,000 each occurrence). Through repetition, mistakes could be reduced and employees could feel more confident starting the job rather than blundering during on-the-job training.

Conclusion

Strivr has worked with a number of other companies such as Fidelity Financial, with whom they've created call-center empathy training. In each case, they tailor the VR training to the company's needs, improving upon existing training content by providing immersion and interactivity from expert instructors on demand. What starts as a proof of concept for a small part of the company is then scaled to the entire company. Much of their content is 360 video and they've figured out a good process for filming then adding interactivity via quiz questions. That said, I expect we'll see 6DOF standalone solutions from them at some point in the future.

ScopeAR

ScopeAR uses both handheld and head mounted AR to help businesses improve efficiencies and cure pain points. Their main focus is in the industrial equipment, manufacturing, and aerospace industries. Although each use case is individualized, their software WorkLink serves as the backbone of their service.

WorkLink connects people remotely through AR enabled devices, and uses AR to apply a kind of powerpoint replacement to the physical world (i.e. visual overlay and instruction walkthrough).

Prince Castle

Prince Castle manufactures and services a large number of industrial food-preparation and related devices. These devices are used at companies like McDonalds.

Sometimes this equipment stops working correctly, and has to be fixed. Before, fixing a malfunctioning machine such as a bun toaster required scheduling a technician to come to the store, diagnose the issue, then repair it.

ScopeAR made it so that when a bun toaster stops working, employees can live-video AR connect to an expert technician using a smartphone or tablet. The technician can walk the employee through a diagnosis, and use AR instructions to make the process easier. For example, the employee may point their smartphone at the bun toaster, and an arrow with text saying "check if light is red" would appear over the machine's on-off indicator.

By using a blend of AR and remote expert instruction, Prince Castle was able to eliminate 50% of service trips compared to before adopting AR. This reduced overall labor cost for repairs by 50-85%. Additionally, first-time correct diagnosis went up to 100%, which I believe can be attributed to the clear and thorough AR instructions.

Without AR, an expert inspecting the machine in person might forget something or only fix the issue temporarily. All this improvement resulted in a happy Prince Castle.

Unilever

Unilever needed help decreasing unscheduled downtime in its ice cream factories. Every second a factory isn't producing goods is money wasted. When equipment stops working unexpectedly, the factory has to have unscheduled downtime until the issue is resolved.

By replacing paper instructions with handheld AR guided instructions Unilever was able to reduce unplanned downtime by 50%. This translated to about $80,000 in savings per month for a single factory. Now they're working to expand the successful AR pilot to the rest of their factories.

Amazing results like this were achieved by directly addressing pain points. 25% of Unilever's ice cream factory repair issues were due to a single issue. Additionally, maintenance issues can result from small things, like forgetting to periodically replace a seal in a cooler. By starting with the most common issue and working outwards, ScopeAR was able to dramatically evolve the effectiveness of Unilever mechanics.

Using AR to label clear, expert-created instructions onto the machinery you are inspecting or repairing offers a huge advantage compared to written instructions. Not only is there more working memory available (since there's no need for 2D to 3D translation), but the opportunity to forget, skip, or miss something decreases dramatically, since it's sequentially programmed and directly labeled.

An additional benefit is that new inspectors and mechanics can be trained and put on the job more quickly. In 5 years, a single factory will lose about 330 years of experience. AR instructions can immortalize and make up for some of that experience. There is also a skills gap between job openings and available skilled labour. AR use can serve as a competitive recruitment tool, since the younger workforce is especially interested in new technology. If you have the choice of working for a company that uses AR, versus one that doesn't, where do you think you'll go? AR can also upskill existing or new workers to handle jobs they otherwise wouldn't be qualified for.

Lockheed Martin

When building spacecraft Lockheed Martin needs to ensure tasks are completed correctly, or astronauts could die and expensive equipment could be destroyed. Using the Hololens AR HMD, ScopeAR has helped them improve efficiency and safety.

For example, when drilling holes in pieces of the spacecraft, Lockheed employees previously had to translate a 2D diagram to 3D. They also had to look back and forth between the image and spacecraft part. With an AR HMD, they are now able to overlay the drill locations directly onto the spacecraft. This resulted in a 35% reduction in labour cost and 85% reduction in training time. On top of this increased efficiency is a decrease in the possibility of costly errors, since the AR HMD can help the driller or their supervisor verify the drilling locations and see if any locations are incorrect or missing.

Lockheed was able to take the same principles and transfer them to another task: setting the correct torque on fasteners. Setting the fastener torques on the Orion heat shield used to take six weeks, but with the help of AR now only takes two. Total labour cost savings equated to 50%. The AR software guides the user through setting each fastener's torque, allowing for batched work (doing every fastener of a certain setting at once), quicker locating, and faster verification.

Applying this methodology to yet another task, Lockheed was able to reduce the touch-labour cost of that activity (placing fasteners) by 93%. What used to take 2 technicians 8 shifts now only takes 1 technician 2.5 hours. Using the authoring software provided by ScopeAR (known as WorkLink Create), it only took 3 hours to create the software that allowed this impressive efficiency gain.

Lockheed's early success with AR has encouraged their other departments to follow suit in adopting its use. Their aerospace division has continued to apply AR guided instructions to their different unique use cases (these three examples are a few of what they are sharing publicly). AR is fundamentally changing the way they work.

Conclusion

ScopeAR has shown that even in early days, AR offers a big impact in communication, training, and workplace efficiency. Their success is based on finding the use cases that benefit most from AR use, and building guided instructions for those specific cases (or allowing their clients to build their own sets of instructions). Combining that with live expert telecommunication has proven a potent combination where applicable.

Osso VR

Osso has deployed a VR surgical training platform. Surgical training and assessment is one of the top value-gain uses of XR since it results in saved lives and healthier patients (contributing to overall workforce productivity and the pricelessness of human lives). VR surgical training has existed in some form for years, but with lowered cost and increased accessibility, that use is starting to scale. Osso started with tethered PC VR headsets, but with the introduction of standalones like the Oculus Quest, it's only a matter of time until all surgeons use VR for training. At Oculus Connect 2019 (the annual VR conference hosted by Facebook), the head of Johnson and Johnson Institute said "we want to make VR available to every surgeon in every hospital around the world". This was said live on stage during the keynote, and with the improved training results it's no surprise. In the summer of 2019 Osso VR already had over a thousand surgeons using their platform monthly. Their userbase includes several medical schools such as UCLA and Harvard, and partnerships with corporate behemoths like Johnson and Johnson who will accelerate adoption further.

As an example of the training experience, a surgeon using Osso would jump into a 6DOF VR operating room. Their assigned procedure is knee replacement, so they pick up a scalpel and make an incision at the knee. Optionally, an expert instructor is in the simulation with them. They (or the program) may comment that the incision was made too low, so the simulation goes back to the prior step and has them make the incision again. This time it was perfect, so they go to the next step of the procedure. Osso uses medical illustrators, so the realism of the 3D models and surgical procedures is very authentic.

But how effective is VR surgeon training? The Imperial College of London conducted an independent study on the effectiveness of VR training for surgeons (the surgery tested was a form of hip replacement). 83% of those who did the VR training could then go into a lab setting and complete the procedure with minimal guidance. 0% of those traditionally trained could.

Another study by UCLA (using Osso VR specifically) found that surgeons in training who used VR as opposed to traditional methods performed the surgery (in a lab environment) 20% faster, completed 38% more of the steps correctly, and scored 230% higher on their surgery test.

These results speak for themselves, and will undoubtedly change the field of surgery training at a rapid pace. Traditionally, surgeons learned by reading books, watching videos, working with cadavers, and observing experienced surgeons work, gradually gaining increased autonomy. However, there are only a limited number of experienced surgeons and cadavers to use, and time with either is expensive. On top of this, observation is no substitute for direct experience, meaning that surgeons performing a new surgery used to essentially be learning a procedure on their first patients (exposing them to increased risk).

VR training fixes both these problems. Since it is software it can be deployed anywhere with any number of devices, greatly limiting the need for cadavers and expert surgeons taking time out of their busy day. Additionally, the training can be repeated indefinitely and mistakes can be pointed out and corrected, with the training allowing practice of the actual procedure rather than observation.

VR can also act as a better form of evaluation for new surgeons or old surgeons on new procedures, to make sure they are ready for a procedure before working on a human patient. New devices and procedures are constantly being brought to the medical field. Surgeons will sometimes avoid procedures that are newer and better because learning it could be dangerous for their early patients until they master the new procedure (so it's easier to stick to what they know). Additionally, even surgeons who do decide to learn new procedures usually have to fly somewhere and get one-off instruction, or use video. With VR new procedures can be taught rapidly and safely as they are developed. Medical device companies have caught on to this and work with Osso to build training for their devices.

In addition to these advantages, a platform like Osso allows more equal access to surgery training across the world. In developing or third world countries, medical expertise is especially hard to come by. VR that's available for only a few hundred dollars could help spread best practices to places that otherwise wouldn't have access.

There are many companies developing surgery training for VR, of which Osso is just one, but I hope you see how impactful VR can be in training situations.

Talespin

Talespin uses both VR and AR to help its enterprise clients. I'll be focusing on the unique aspects of their VR work since as of early 2020 their AR offerings are not available.

Human Resources, Communication, and Leadership

"Soft skills" such as leadership and communication are infamously difficult to train and measure, yet widely recognized as one of the most important skills for employee development. To show VR's potential in this space Talespin created a demo which we'll call "Firing Barry".

In "Firing Barry", you are immersed in an office environment and sit down with Barry, a 60 year old employee who you've been tasked with firing. Barry has realistic rendering and facial expressions, and will react to the decisions you make. You're given multiple choices at certain points in the conversation, and using speech recognition have to actually say them out loud.

Barry will react with emotion to your responses, but if you choose the "wrong" response you will be told so and have to restart the simulation. "Firing Barry" is interesting because it takes a stressful situation that is hard to train for and allows you to practice it, becoming confident in your ability to stay on task and be as respectful as possible. Barry's realism gives you a true emotional response that would be difficult to replicate in an in-person roleplay (unless your coworkers are great actors or you hire a professional in-person coach). Additionally, VR lets you practice in a safe space without the discomfort of peers judging your roleplay.

Traditional roleplay training also lacks scalability. With "Firing Barry" you have something that is repeatable infinitely and on-demand to as many places as you want, while with in-person roleplay each session is different and dependent on the acting of peers or a hired trainer. In person training also requires everyone to meet at the same time.

Roleplay with peers is more awkward, with poorly faked emotion if any. Self-censorship abounds when in person, while practicing alone in VR lets you try different tactics without fear of reprisal.

Another benefit of VR is the potential for data feedback. For example, you could track someone's eye and head movements between firing a male or female coworker and point out certain biases that emerge. Alternatively, you can track metrics such as how many tries it takes to successfully complete the simulation, allowing you to tweak the training.

Barry is ultimately a demo and not actually sold to companies. However, using similar technology (VR, realistic humans, voice recognition, and AI) many companies have worked with Talespin to create company-specific training. Most of these use cases are targeted towards "difficult conversations" and other types of managerial conversations. For example, they might create a scenario where a customer has had a bad experience and you need to rebuild trust with them. Another example: practicing rapport building with a sales lead.

Unfortunately the specifics of these trainings are not public, but it's clear that many companies are looking for VR soft skills training specific to their needs. Talespin's website has a list of 31 different roleplay scenarios that could be made across Human Resources, Leadership, Sales, and Customer Service training just for a start. This includes domains such as public speaking practice, cold calling, and conflict resolution to name a few.

Insurance

One of Talespin's biggest clients has been the insurance industry, starting with Farmers Insurance. Using 6DOF VR, insurance agents can be trained to inspect a house for potential issues without ever leaving the office. The locations agents need to train in (i.e. peoples' homes) are not available except for a pre-configured training house, which requires travel, is fairly expensive, and has limited time available. With VR, agents can be given many house variations to inspect on demand.

For example, an agent enters a VR house and is tasked with finding any water leaks. They move around the house, clicking on the leaks they find while a timer counts down. Doing A/B testing for agents trained with VR vs traditionally, Talespin saw an increase of 20% in decision accuracy. This translates to significant savings considering the average claim is $7,000-10,000.

Talespin's newest software runs on the Oculus Quest, making use of its hand tracking to remove the need for controllers. Users simply press buttons or objects in the environment with their hands. The switchover to controllerless standalone VR made Talespin's training simpler, cheaper, and more mobile for customers.

Conclusion

These are just some of Talespin's uses of VR, but they show how VR can be used for training and practice whether in soft or hard skills.

IrisVR

Using multi-user 6DOF VR, IrisVR's Prospect software helps the building industry improve efficiency, specificity, and collaboration. IrisVR's software is available on both tethered VR (Oculus Rift and SteamVR headsets) as well as the Oculus Quest.

Prospect allows construction professionals (such as architects) to import 3D models into a VR scene. These models can come directly from the programs these professionals already use, such as SketchUp, Revit, Rhino, Grasshopper, Navisworks, FBX and OBJ exporting programs, and more. Once the model is imported, it can be viewed in VR as either an individual or group with networked avatars (i.e. you can see each others' head and hands movement and talk with your voice).

This is useful because it allows architects to view their creations in first person at the appropriate scale and perspective. You can experience your building before a single brick is laid. Inconsistencies or errors in the designs are also easier to spot than on a flat screen.

Having multiple users in the environment allows remote collaboration and immediate context-based collaboration. For example, pointing to a doorway and saying, "this needs to be moved two inches to the left" then placing that as a note on the door. It's also great as a client-feedback tool during design reviews. If you're spending ten million dollars to build a building, being able to look at the building and give direct feedback based on the feel is invaluable. Previously, this kind of feedback was achieved through physical models or flat screen viewing. VR's perspective offers a huge advantage.

IrisVR works with a large number of clients in the building industry, such as SHoP Architects (who designed Brooklyn's Barclays Center). SHoP claims VR helped them improve client communication and compress time spent in design review. They believe this has in turn helped them get additional work with clients.

Conclusion

Although exact metrics are hard to come by, it is clear that VR is providing qualitative value to the construction industry in the form of clearer and more confident design. Quantitative value also appears to be present in the form of less money spent on travel, more efficient implementation of design, and increased revenue from clients.

A Drop in the Ocean

These companies are just a few examples of successful XR use in enterprise. There are well over a hundred businesses using XR, with thousands more to come. If you want to explore more companies and use cases, the VRAR Association has a large list known as "the Directory". Hopefully this chapter has convinced you that XR can be implemented in enterprise with today's technology for valuable return on investment (ROI). Whether your needs are in training, productivity, safety, advertising or more, VR and AR can provide massive benefit when applied correctly. As we continue to develop best practices and experiment, XR will become a common workplace tool.

CHAPTER 4:
XR SOFTWARE DESIGN

This chapter focuses on information that will help you implement effective XR from a more technical standpoint. We'll cover all the ways I'm currently aware of to avoid sim sickness through design, then give an overview of the most important optimization and visual improvement tips. If you're in no way involved in the technical or design side of creating XR content you may decide to skip to the next chapter.

Tips for Avoiding Sim Sickness

As we talked about earlier in the book, modern VR hardware is capable of avoiding sim sickness in the vast majority of people. The software ultimately determines whether a user feels discomfort, and is the area designers and developers have the most control over.

Motion Sickness is a subset of Sim Sickness that is very common, so we'll start with some design tips to either remove or reduce motion sickness in VR apps. Then we'll talk about other sim-sickness-reducing tips to keep in mind when designing VR apps.

The focus for this section is on VR because AR has a different relationship with sim sickness. Most AR apps don't move you through virtual space, and keep you grounded in physical reality. That said, many of these tips probably apply to AR should you design your AR apps closer to that of VR. Also note, I've personally never worn an AR HMD without getting sim sickness, probably due to the hardware's low frame rate and tracking latency (although uncomfortable ergonomics may also be to blame). Handheld AR usually doesn't cause sim sickness since the field of view is so small.

I expect AR frame rate and tracking to improve to the point of being comfortable like VR within a year or two of this book's release. However, since writing these principles in the context of AR would be guesswork (there are still too many confounding factors and the hardware is changing so fast), I've decided to focus on the principles from a VR perspective to keep things clear and in the realm of what is well tested.

Artificial Locomotion

Any disconnect between a user's proprioceptive system (i.e. their body's sense of motion) and what they see is capable of causing motion sickness. How then do users move around in a VR app?

We'll start out by discussing locomotion (i.e. movement) techniques that essentially cause no motion sickness. Because most enterprise users aren't trying to maximize gaming immersion, I recommend these "full-comfort" locomotion techniques as the default for most enterprise apps.

If these "full-comfort" solutions don't fit your use case or you want users who aren't as sensitive to have different options, I've included a number of locomotion styles and tips that can reduce motion sickness while having freer movement. It's important to keep in mind that not everyone suffers from sim sickness, and that it's a spectrum where increased exposure can reduce its effects.

Teleport

It turns out that if you instantly move a player from one location to another (known as Teleporting) they don't experience motion sickness. This makes sense because our brains don't recognize teleporting as movement. Our minds aren't used to the experience of suddenly shifting several meters away without any vection (i.e. sensation of movement), so we can move in VR very comfortably by teleporting.

In some ways, sim sickness can be thought of as the uncanny valley effect of immersion. If our brains' expectations of reality don't line up with what we see in the VR headset, our brain thinks something is wrong. However, if we completely trick the brain into thinking the immersive experience is real, or do something that our brain knows is not real, we generally won't get sick.

Free Teleport

One of the most popular ways to implement teleportation is to use a laser beam with a parabolic arc attached to the hand. The user aims their hand (and thus the laser) where they want to go, see an indicator on the floor of where they will arrive, then either press (or in most cases release) the button to teleport. The user then appears at the spot indicated.

Some developers make the teleport happen instantly with no transition. The danger of this is that it can be a bit jarring, and if you allow rapid teleports the illusion of motion can be strong enough to still cause motion sickness. A common trick to avoid this is a quick fade to black then back up. The fade happens very quickly and is barely perceivable, but gives the brain a transition cue to make teleporting less jarring. You can also set a limit on how many times a user can teleport in a set amount of time, but need to be careful with this as it can be frustrating for players who want to move quickly.

Another solution is the Dash Teleport. Instead of instantly moving the user, Dash Teleport moves the user very quickly over time, often with some combination of the motion-reduction tips from later in this chapter. It gives users the feeling of traversing through the space, which can lead to them being more aware of their new surroundings. The motion is so fast that our brains have trouble recognizing it as motion. Although this technique works for many people, it can still cause issues for some, so you need to be careful using it as your default "comfort" option.

Free teleport has become an industry standard for apps that need a comfortable-for-everyone option combined with the ability to move freely throughout a VR environment.

Waypoint Teleport

Some apps need to restrict user movement to certain locations. In these instances, it is common to use a teleport waypoint system. Essentially, the user can see indicators for specific locations they can teleport, rather than being able to teleport anywhere with a laser arc. The indicator could be in the form of a glowing light, a 3D icon, or any number of other representations.

For example, you may have the teleportable locations light up or show an indicator when you look at them. Then you press a button or keep looking for a few seconds to teleport to the new location. Instead you may give the user a laser pointer on their hand, and allow them to click on a teleport location icon to go there.

Although waypoint teleport is more restrictive, it can ensure your user goes to the places you want, and in some cases, sees the start of the location how you want them to see it.

Room Scale and Scene-Based

Another option for avoiding any motion sickness is to never move the user artificially. "Room scale" is a term used to describe a VR experience where the user can move around their environment physically in 360 degrees. Because the motion is one-to-one (due to the great tracking), no vestibular disconnect occurs. The motion you are seeing reflects the motion of your own body, and thus of your own inner ear.

Obviously, this can be fairly restrictive. The recommended minimum space for a room scale VR experience is 2 meters by 1.5 meters. This means that the user in the virtual world is also somewhat restricted to that amount of space. If you need the user to use more virtual space, you can do so by using a larger physical space. Such "warehouse scale" VR is possible with the current technology, and can make sense for certain use cases, but is also potentially expensive. How many companies have a large empty room they can use for this purpose?

A way to get around limited space is to design for room scale but allow transitions (or teleports) to specific locations. For example, if you are training someone at McDonalds how to flip burgers in the kitchen, but then want them to practice with the cash register out front, the scene can transition the user from the kitchen to the register counter via a button on a menu, a teleport waypoint, or completion of the burger flipping lesson.

With larger spaces, it is also possible to use "redirected walking", a technique that allows a user to feel like they are walking in a straight line when in actuality they are turning. Redirected walking can make a warehouse space feel like it has infinite size. The bare minimum space required to use redirected walking is about 6x6 meters, but more is preferable. Tricks can also be used to make a smaller space seem bigger using turning.

If you are going to constrain your user to only physical space locomotion within a scene, but need the user to access objects outside of their physical space, telekinesis can be a useful method.

In apps that make use of telekinesis, the user points or looks at an object that is distant (sometimes with a laser pointer or cursor), then the object either glows or has some indicator pop up to show that it is highlighted. Pressing the grab button then floats the object into the user's hand, or allows them to move it in relation to how their hand moves. Sometimes a trackpad or joystick is used to control how close or far the object moves from the hand. This technique requires more training and practice than just picking objects up naturally with your hands, so I'd hesitate to use it in an enterprise setting, but it can be an interesting solution.

Smooth Locomotion (reducing sim sickness for other movement techniques)

Whatever your reason, you may decide teleport and room scale don't work for what you're trying to accomplish with VR. Gaming and narrative uses especially can benefit from smoother locomotion techniques (i.e. locomotion that involves vection). If that's the case, there are still an array of tricks you can employ to make users more comfortable.

Vection Reduction

Vection is the feeling of movement produced by visual stimulation. Since vection in VR doesn't match what our bodies (specifically our vestibular system) feel, it can make us experience discomfort (i.e. sim sickness).

One way to reduce discomfort from vection is to use it sparingly. Perhaps the user performs most of their tasks from a standstill, and only locomotes through the environment to go to a new activity.

Reducing movement speed also reduces vection (to a certain point). There is actually a balance between how long you experience vection and vection magnitude. The traditional advice is that if you move the user more slowly, they will experience less discomfort than moving them more quickly, and this is often true.

However, as discussed with Sprint Teleport, there is a speed above which our brains don't recognize motion the same way, and thus if that threshold is achieved, faster speed may be better. Unfortunately, it's not clear cut because this "threshold" is more likely a spectrum, and that spectrum is different for every individual person.

It may be possible that moving someone at a speed of 6m/s for 10 seconds is more comfortable in the long run than moving someone 3m/s for 20 seconds, because even though the vection magnitude is greater for 6m/s, the user experiences vection for double the time at 3m/s. If possible, you probably want to allow user movement speed to be adjustable in settings, since different speeds are comfortable for each person. You also will want to test different speeds and see what feels good for the majority of people.

When I first started in VR, I used the Oculus recommended 1.4m/s for walking in a game I was making. It was very comfortable for my short experience. However, users repeatedly reported frustration with how slow the movement felt. If you're going to have smooth locomotion, you probably want to avoid user frustration (and wasting user time) by employing as fast a movement speed as comfortable, along with the techniques later in this section.

Acceleration / Deceleration Reduction

Acceleration and deceleration are far more problematic than vection when it comes to motion induced sim sickness. To rephrase, changes in motion are more uncomfortable than motion itself.

The general rule of thumb is that shorter periods of acceleration are better than longer periods. This means that instant acceleration to a set speed and instant deceleration can be more comfortable than gradual speeding up and slowing down. It's important to keep in mind that changes in direction constitute a velocity change, meaning that if the app requires strafing (moving side to side) via artificial locomotion, the user is experiencing constant velocity change.

Traditional console game thumbstick movement uses variable speed, meaning that the user can have a speed anywhere from 0 to their max speed in any direction (by pushing the thumbstick in that direction by a variable amount). This finely-variable speed of movement is generally less comfortable than quick or instant acceleration to a max speed.

So, where possible you want to make your velocity changes instant or very quick (if trying to minimize movement discomfort).

Perceived Movement Reduction

How much movement we perceive is affected by the environment around us. So, by reducing movement cues in our scene, we can lower discomfort.

For example, how tall a user is affects how fast the ground seems to be moving, as well as how much of our vision is taken up by the moving ground. Placing a user close to the ground is not recommended for comfort.

In VR development, the user's view is called a "camera". One of the popular implementations for a user camera is to set its height from the floor equal to that of the user (so the user appears as tall in VR as in physical life). This is generally a good idea for reasons other than sim comfort, such as increased immersion, being able to reach objects on the floor, and balance. In this case you are powerless to change physical height.

However, there are also times where for the sake of design consistency you need the user to be a certain height (or a height within certain bounds). For times like this, you want to choose a height that feels comfortable for a majority of your demographic, but that isn't too close to the ground.

The floor is just one surface that can cause perceived motion. If you are out in an open space, you'll often see a skybox, which doesn't move as you get closer to it (since a skybox will always appear the same from any distance). Objects that are very distant also don't appear to move much as you move. It's safe to conclude then that the most comfortable types of environments are those where you're in an open space without walls or a ceiling.

Once you're inside, walls and ceiling can increase your sense of movement, since they change in your periphery. That said, you can still have a comfortable experience with an indoor environment. Just avoid tight enclosed spaces where possible.

A good example of this principle in action can come from Echo Arena, a 0-gravity VR game on 6DOF headsets. While playing the tutorial, which constitutes a series of narrow rooms, people report increased motion sickness compared to the game's lobby and play arena, which take place in much more open and expansive environments despite being indoors.

Peripheral Blinders (Field of View Limiting)

A common technique used to reduce motion sickness with smooth locomotion is the use of peripheral blinders. Essentially, when a user moves, the edges of their vision fade to black. When the user stops moving, the black at the edge of their view disappears. This probably works because the blinders block or reduce the motion our peripheral vision sees. Lessening of field of view that perceives motion is one of the most surefire ways to reduce discomfort.

Although this technique can reduce motion sickness in most people, some report that it increases discomfort. Whether or not this is the case (the perceived discomfort may be worse without it), the technique can be implemented to varying degrees of intrusiveness. Generally, the more pronounced and immersion-breaking the black rim, the more effective at preventing motion discomfort.

Thus, there is a fine line to walk between keeping users immersed, and keeping them physically comfortable. Users who don't suffer from sim sickness generally hate peripheral blinders, and even those who need it will complain if it is too pronounced, so be careful with this technique, possibly making it an option that can be disabled.

Movement in Viewpoint Direction

If the user is looking in the direction they are moving, they will experience less discomfort than moving in a different direction from where they are looking.

A common implementation of smooth locomotion for VR is to press a button (or the joystick / trackpad forward), and have the user move in the direction they are looking. For games with gravity, the up /

down of the head is ignored. This is in contrast to moving forward, then allowing the head to turn freely after you've started moving, without affecting your direction. That said, there are still plenty of apps that allow you to move in directions other than where you are looking (including strafing side to side and backing up).

Design-wise, you want to encourage your users to move in the direction they are looking, or look in the direction they are moving since other movements will increase discomfort. Perhaps instead of allowing artificial strafing, make it so the user has to physically move side to side in the VR app. A great example of this is the game Pistol Whipped, which moves the user slowly forwards (in one set direction) through an environment, but encourages the user to dodge side to side with their physical body.

Give User Control of Movement

As much as possible, it's better to allow users to control their artificial locomotion rather than moving them unexpectedly. When a user anticipates that a control input (such as a button press) will move them, sim sickness is reduced. Although the mechanism for this is not fully understood, it's plausible to believe that when our brains expect motion to occur, the proprioceptive disconnect that occurs from artificial locomotion is not as unexpected, and so not as uncomfortable. Ultimately, what matters most is that giving users control of their own movement definitely increases comfort, and possibly allows them to build a mental connection between the input and the motion (which as we'll talk about later, can build resistance over time).

Roller-coaster VR simulators are an example of how to reliably get people who aren't immune sick, because in addition to the fast speed and many turns, the user has no control over the motion happening to them. The visual indicator of the track can provide some expectation of movement, but because the coaster goes so fast, that movement is generally not expected the same way a button-press-to-response is.

Author's Note: Please, stop showing new VR users roller coaster apps. They are a terrible intro to VR, especially on a 3DOF headset.

Provide Cues for Non-User-Controlled Locomotion

When the user has to be moved without their own input, providing sound and haptic cues can reduce discomfort by giving their brains an action-reaction expectation.

For example in Echo Arena (the 0-gravity Oculus game) you have control of your movement most of the time. However, if you hit your head on a wall while flying, you bounce off it. Usually when you hit your head, it isn't an intentional thing, and so is not an anticipated change in movement. Despite this, bouncing off something in Echo Arena feels fairly comfortable.

This is because when you hit your head on something in the game, a distinct "thump" sound is played, coinciding with a haptic rumble on both your hand controllers. The result is a visceral "thump" of your head that you instantly recognize, turning a situation of unexpected velocity change into "oh dang, I just hit my head".

This is the kind of presence and embodiment that VR can provide. Increasing our sense of embodiment can make our brains more comfortable in VR. So, wherever possible make unexpected direction changes feel like an expected result of something within the VR simulation. Sound and haptics can go a long way to increasing immersion and building brain expectations.

Consistent Orientation

We've talked about artificial movement, but what about rotation? Artificial rotation is in some cases the most sim sickness inducing experience that can occur (dropped frames and bad hardware can be as bad or worse).

Imagine you are sitting here reading this book, then the whole world starts spinning around you. This is the same experience of smoothly turning the user in VR, and for many people it's an instantly bad time. That said, I'll remind once again that comfort is a spectrum, with some users able to turn with traditional first-person shooter joystick controls just fine.

How then do we turn the user comfortably? Well, one sure-to-work option is to have the user turn their head physically. This can work very well for standing or room scale experiences, but fails if your user is seated. Another option is to use peripheral blinders whenever the user turns, but this solution isn't perfect.

You could design your app so that the user never needs to turn. My first few VR prototypes used this method, but it was admittedly lackluster. People don't like to feel restricted, and designing a forward-only facing VR app with no artificial turning makes it very hard and situational to use this technique. It can certainly work; games like Space Pirate Trainer and my own Meme Dragons drop waves of enemies in front of you to shoot, making it so you don't ever need to turn. Users don't miss the turning in this case because they don't have a reason to turn.

But, as soon as your experience takes place in a 3D world with free movement, turning becomes necessary. So far, the industry has come up with one effective solution: snap turning.

Snap Turning

Snap Turning is a technique where flicking a joystick or touchpad right or left instantly turns the user a pre-set number of degrees (often 45-90). There is no acceleration, because the frame instantly changes to 45 degrees turn right or left. This trick appears to be a very comfortable way to turn for most people. However, it can be fairly jarring for new users, and has a bit of a learning curve. Because it breaks the smooth motion we'd expect from reality, it can also reduce immersion.

That said, with practice users can learn to quickly reorient themselves after a snap turn, building the muscle-memory expectation of "if I press the stick this direction, I'll turn 45 degrees and be looking over here". If the degree increments are too small, turning can be frustrating and appear like motion, which defeats the whole purpose.

Snap Turning is comfortable and pervasive enough that I'd recommend it as an option for any VR app that uses artificial turning (since for many people, other artificial turning methods are untenable). Just keep in mind, users who can handle smooth turning usually prefer it.

Avoid Pitch and Roll

Turning around to look behind you is a turn on the Y-axis, which is known as "yaw". Turns on the Z-axis (i.e. somersaulting forwards) are known as "pitch", and turns on the X-axis (i.e. a cartwheel) are known as "roll". The term "stick yaw" is commonly used in the VR and gaming industry in reference to stick / trackpad turning, which we talked about in the last section. Smooth yaw turning is already very uncomfortable, but pitch and roll are even more so.

Living our day to day lives, we rarely experience significant pitch and roll, and our experience of it is almost entirely initiated by our heads. The few exceptions are events like riding a roller coaster or getting shoved to the ground, events that are generally disorienting. Astronauts undergo significant training to prepare for the common pitch and roll of 0-gravity, and even still often have to adjust to being in space before getting over initial nausea (usually taking drugs like dramamine).

So, to create a comfortable experience you should avoid artificial turning in the pitch and roll directions. Obviously, if you want to create a realistic flight simulator this is not possible, but the vast majority of experiences don't require pitch or roll.

Fixed Horizon

Related to the pitch and roll discussion, having a fixed horizon can help ground the user and reduce discomfort. If the user is floating in a void of space with no clear horizon, they can become disoriented and feel increased sim sickness. The same thing can occur if the horizon starts moving.

Visible skyboxes are the easiest way to accomplish this. A skybox appears the same no matter how far the user is away from it, providing a consistent far-away grounding reference for our eyes. Other far off non-moving pieces of geometry (such as a wall) can also provide this.

An example of breaking this tip would be to have a massive castle rise directly in front of a user, or to put them in an elevator where they can see the walls moving past. Space sims with yaw and roll break this tip as well, since the horizon spins depending on what direction you turn.

Fixed Focal Point

If your vision is focused on a specific object and able to follow it, some motion sickness can be reduced. For example, when driving we are usually focused on the car in front of us or the horizon, which barely move relative to the road. If you were to watch the road directly below you instead you would feel much more discomfort.

Another example comes from Echo Arena, where you chase a disc around a 0-gravity environment. Even though you are moving quickly through the environment with artificial locomotion, much of your visual focus is on the disc or the other players around you. You're so focused on a fixed object, you barely notice the vection of your peripheral vision.

HUD and Cockpits (Fixed Objects and FOV motion reduction)

A heads-up display (HUD) constitutes a user interface (UI) made up of elements fixed to a user's face. For example, a racing simulator might attach your car's speed to the lower right of your vision so that you can check your speed with a glance. As you turn your head, the UI stays in the same relative location, and so appears to never move.

Having too many visual elements fixed to your head can be uncomfortable. However, subtle use of HUD elements can decrease discomfort by providing a constant fixed reference point.

For example, Echo Arena uses subtle UI images attached to the face to give the user the feeling that they are wearing a helmet. The presence of these images reduces sim sickness (probably because of reduced perception on vection, but the reason is not fully understood). Generally I'd recommend keeping fixed UI elements to the peripheral vision rather than areas of the visual field where you spend most of your time focusing. However, this is just a rule of thumb.

As with the peripheral blinders we talked about, limiting how much of the vection we perceive can also reduce sim sickness. An effective way to do this can be through the use of cockpits, which block part of our field of view from seeing movement. The feeling of being in a vehicle may also contribute to tricking our brain into accepting artificial locomotion.

While piloting a spaceship in the VR version of the game No Man's Sky, the cockpit takes up much of your vision and there are HUD elements fixed to the viewport, helping to reduce sim sickness. Other games like Vox Machina, a mech piloting game, use similar tactics.

Using Embodied Movement

When we involve our body in artificial movement, sim sickness appears to be reduced. This isn't fully understood, but it's likely because moving our physical body tricks our brain into thinking our physical actions are causing physical movement, despite the movement being virtual.

One to one hand movement to body movement seems to work very well. This "climbing" or "crawling" movement works by having users press a "grab" button, then move their hand in the direction opposite to where they want to go. As you move your hand down, your body (and with it your head) moves up. Move the hand right, and you go left. This movement behaves like how we'd expect our actions to occur in the physical world (if you pull yourself up a rock wall, you bring your hands closer to your body, which moves your body up).

Echo Arena makes use of this trick, allowing you to climb around the environment and throw yourself into 0-G off of walls and other objects. A parkour racing game mode in Rec Room uses a similar technique to allow you to climb up walls.

Another embodied movement technique is "arm running". Users pump their arms as if they are running, and this causes them to move forward through the environment. The games Sprint Vector and Climbey are good examples of this.

So, it appears that connecting physical movement to artificial locomotion in a natural way increases our immersion and stops our brains from freaking out as much. These are just two methods of embodied virtual locomotion that the industry has thought of so far. There are still plenty of possibilities waiting to be discovered or popularized.

Reducing Overstimulation

VR environments can be overstimulating, meaning the user experiences mental fatigue from the complexity of how much is going on. Additionally, high detail can be lost to the VR display, instead creating increased vection.

If you wanted to design an environment that would be as uncomfortable as possible, you would use lots of bright colors and color variation. The geometry would be very complex, with textures (aka color arrangements) that contained a plethora of fine details and lines.

Very bright colors can be exhausting for users, so it's better to use a tone that isn't too bright (so neon green as a major part of the environment is probably out). This is a common design principle even outside of VR for the same reason, but VR emphasises the eye strain.

Similarly, in any design too much complexity can make it difficult to see the shapes of the art clearly. Too many lines or colors can make an object difficult to parse (i.e. make out). In VR this problem is exacerbated because of relatively low pixels-per-degrees compared to flat monitors. Very detailed art ends up looking messy and unclear because there aren't enough pixels to display it.

Even with better displays, too many lines and color / shape changes increase the feeling of vection when a user is artificially moving. The most comfortable VR environments use simple geometry with relatively few colors, but that doesn't mean they have to be unsophisticated. You can achieve high realism without making the 3D objects overly complex. Many developers prefer using cartoony art for VR because it's easier to make it look good.

"VR Legs" (Repeated Exposure)

Repeated use of VR and artificial locomotion can increase resistance to sim sickness. People can earn their "VR legs" by a combination of persistence and gradual intensity increase. Gained resistance to the effects of sim sickness are not overly surprising. About half of astronauts sent to the space station experience 0-gravity sickness their first few days. At first their vestibular system is very confused. However, as they live their lives in 0-gravity and gain familiarity with it their body starts to relax. VR can work the same way. However, it is unclear what frequency of use improves comfort at what rate and for how long the resistance lasts; it is definitely variable for each person. You may do a VR gaming or training binge one week and have an iron stomach by the end, but if you then stay away from VR for a few days and go back, how resistant will you be? This is not well understood.

Relying on users to get experience with VR vestibular disconnect is an uncertain business. One method could be to start a user with a very comfortable experience, then slowly graduate them to more and more extreme forms of artificial locomotion. However, many people don't want to feel the effects of sim sickness, and would rather not use VR than train their bodies to be able to use your app.

Generally it's advised to not fight through the discomfort and to instead take a break when you notice it. Doing otherwise can result in a very unpleasant experience and potentially form an automatic association in a person's mind between VR use and that unpleasant feeling.

I think where possible it is best to offer options for users. This allows them to build resistance at their own pace, and allows users with immunity to jump right into the style of movement they desire.

Final Thoughts

When tourists go up in a plane that simulates 0-gravity (which was used to train astronauts), about 60% experience motion sickness.

Should we then expect about 60% of the population to be susceptible to the discomfort?

This chapter contains many tricks for avoiding motion sickness in VR, and these are only the practical ones I've seen so far. As the industry develops and more experimentation is done, we'll probably find more! In the long run, if kids start to use VR at a relatively early age, they may gain immunity to vestibular disconnect just like kids who grow up playing high-action video games gain resistance to its motion sickness effects.

3D Optimization

If you don't hit an XR headset's target frame rate consistently without fail, it doesn't matter how careful your comfort design is. People who are susceptible will feel the effects of sim sickness when frame rate is low or inconsistent. PC connected headsets allow the user to control their computing horsepower, while mobile standalone headsets have a set capability. Here are some optimization tips to keep in mind when designing or developing for XR systems, to ensure you hit your target frame rate and have crisp visuals.

Reducing Scene Weight

There are a few factors of an XR scene that generally act as the bottleneck for computer performance. By keeping these bottlenecks in mind, you can design and develop XR software that achieves consistent framerate.

First, some 101 basics on 3D rendering. In the vast majority of current 3D engines, 3D models are made up of a mesh and a texture.

The mesh can be thought of as the geometry of the model, while the texture is the skin or coloration. Meshes are made up of many triangles connected together. The corners of each triangle are known as vertices (a single point is a vertex). So, each 3D mesh is essentially made up of vertex points that are connected together into triangles. Textures are 2D images that then get mapped onto the mesh, giving the 3D model coloration and other detail.

Computers also have two main types of processor that are used for XR: a CPU and GPU. The CPU runs operations in a linear order and tells the GPU what to do (as well as running other calculations), while the GPU runs calculations in a parallel manner and is optimized for certain kinds of calculations. Knowing whether your app is "CPU or GPU bound" can allow you to optimize where needed. Sometimes your GPU is struggling but your CPU isn't even breaking a sweat, and the reverse can be true.

Triangles and Vertices (Polygons)

A major bottleneck is the triangle count and vertex count of your 3D geometry. This is often referred to as a "polygon count" or "poly count". Keep in mind that most modern 3D engines break all polygons into triangles, since triangle calculations have been well optimized in the computer hardware and engine software. Vertex count is usually the best metric to use when judging the weight (i.e. processing needs) of a scene's 3D geometry.

The more vertices you use in a model, the smoother and more detailed you can make the edges of the mesh. The film studio Pixar uses millions of vertices in their models to achieve very smooth and detailed animation in their films. However, Pixar pre-renders each frame of their films, meaning they don't need their 3D models to render in real time. Their renders can take anywhere from seconds to hours depending on the computer. XR, in contrast, requires each frame to render in under 20 milliseconds, or even less depending on the refresh rate.

So, when developing for XR, make sure to check the triangle / vertex count of models you use, and where possible reduce their complexity. Good textures can make low-poly models appear more detailed than they actually are, and often geometric detail in a mesh is not required for the intended effect.

The Descrimination Threshold is the point at which users can't tell the difference between two visual stimuli and it can be tested by showing a group of people two models (a high poly and low poly version) then asking them which is more detailed. If 50% choose each model, the test subjects can't tell any difference between the two models, so the increased level of detail is irrelevant. If 75% choose the correct model, about half of the people can't tell the difference, which Oculus recommends as the metric to use.

As a general rule of thumb, it's recommended to use less than 1 million vertices for PC VR headsets and less than 100,000 vertices for mobile VR headsets, although that number is dependent on other factors and will likely go up as computing hardware improves.

Polygon complexity is mainly handled by the GPU, so if your app's GPU is on fire, polygon count should be one of the first things you check.

Draw Calls

Probably the biggest bottleneck on the CPU side is draw calls. A draw call is an instruction the CPU sends to the GPU telling it what to process in the 3D scene. You can think of a draw call as the letter a manager at a company sends to his team telling everyone what to do. Preparing and sending those instructions can take a fair amount of time.

"Becky, I need you to pick up 3 bags of coffee from the store. John, I need you to think of a name for our new product. Chris, I need you to set up the conference room for a meeting at 6pm." Now imagine preparing a list of a hundred of these instructions and sending an individual letter for each one.

A unique draw call needs to be sent for each texture-material pair in the scene. A material tells the renderer how to display a given object via a component called a shader, while the texture is just a 2D image the material uses. Notice, however, that a draw call isn't needed for each 3D model. As long as a model shares the same material and texture as another model, their draw calls can be batched into one, saving significant CPU processing.

A common way to achieve this is to create a giant texture, called a texture atlas, for all the objects in your scene that use the same material. For each individual object, only the portion of the texture atlas relevant to it is used. This is done through the use of UV mapping, which basically tells a 3D model which parts of a texture line up with where on the 3D mesh.

With texture atlasing, a scene that would otherwise take hundreds of draw calls can instead take only a few. A general rule of thumb limit for PC VR is 1000 draw calls, with mobile VR best kept under 100 draw calls. However, like with polygons this is just a general guideline and not a hard rule.

A Note on Ray Tracing

Ray tracing is a new method of 3D rendering that is up and coming. Instead of the traditional method of 3D rendering, which relies on math approximate lighting, ray tracing seeks to simulate exactly how light works (i.e. shooting millions-billions of rays of light and having them bounce off objects). As of now, ray tracing is more computationally expensive than traditional rendering and struggles to be viable for VR.

However, the technology is still very new, and I expect it to garner popularity in the coming decade. The realism achievable by ray tracing is incredible. Because it simulates how we perceive light with our own eyes, it essentially IS real. I saw a pre-rendered video demo of ray tracing in a 3DOF VR headset and felt intense presence beyond anything I'd seen with other computer-generated imagery. Definitely keep an eye on ray tracing's viability, as many new GPUs are including optimizations for the technique.

Warning About Tile Renderers

Some mobile VR headsets (such as the Oculus Quest) use a special processing component called a Tile Renderer. Tile Renderers break their rendering of a single frame into many tiles.

Without getting into too much detail, the main thing to keep in mind when working with Tile Renderers is that multiple rendering passes are extra expensive. The practical takeaway from this is that post-processing effects should generally be avoided on a Tile Renderer, as should any shaders or lighting techniques that require multiple passes (such as real time shadows). Baking your lights is also generally a good idea (i.e. you precompute your lighting rather than having it processed every frame).

You can of course defy this advice if you have the processing budget and know what you're doing.

Visual Improvement Tips

Anti-Aliasing

Due to VR's relatively low pixels-per-degree, visuals are especially prone to aliasing. Aliasing is a jagged edge on lines that should be straight caused by how pixels are arranged on a screen. It looks bad and can cause headaches, so is best mitigated.

Luckily, Anti-Aliasing is an available feature present in most 3D engines. Anti-Aliasing smoothes out the jagged lines and can be set to varying degrees of smoothening (2x, 4x, 8x etc). Anti-Aliasing comes with some computational cost, but is usually well worth it in some form. Best of all, making use of it is usually as simple as turning it on.

Mipmaps

Another way to improve your XR visuals is with the use of mipmaps. Mipmaps are pre-computed lower resolution versions of your textures. Aliasing generally occurs when the image you are trying to render doesn't have enough pixels to smoothly show details. Imagine trying to render the Mona Lisa in 100 pixels. The pixels rendered would seem nonsensical and randomly change depending on your viewing angle moment to moment.

Mipmaps fix this problem by switching the texture of a 3D object depending on how far away it is. If you're super far away from your Mona Lisa it will show the pre-computed version with less detail, and so less aliasing.

Many 3D engines allow you to automatically generate and use mipmaps by checking a few boxes. They do increase the amount of memory your app requires, but the tradeoff in visual improvement is usually worth it.

Turn Off Specular Highlights

Specular highlights are the bright spot on shiny objects when they are lit up. If you notice your XR visuals shimmering even though you've turned on anti-aliasing and mipmaps, check to see if turning off specular highlights on your materials fixes the issue.

I'm not 100% sure why specular highlights are so problematic in XR, but from what I've read it seems like there might be an issue with the specular equations not taking the stereoscopic view into account.

Conclusion

These are just a handful of tips for improving your XR experiences. If you want to explore topics like these in more detail, I recommend checking out the Oculus Developer Blog and my own blog at moduXR.com

CHAPTER 5: HARDWARE

VR is Now

For the past six years I've worked in the XR industry building a plethora of apps, creating development curriculum, training developers, and writing books. In 2014, VR was here as an exciting emerging technology that was clearly here to stay. The clunkiness and lack of compelling apps was understood to be a temporary reality on VR's rise to greatness. Compared to the VR boom and bust of the 90s there were two new factors that gave us that confidence.

First, VR tech had reached that wow and comfort factor that guaranteed a hardcore user base and blew the mind of many who tried it for the first time. Sure, many of those who tried it were skeptical of its commercial viability, and many felt nauseous because of poor software, but it certainly got people talking and core users playing.

Second, Facebook acquired Oculus, the leader in the VR consumer hardware space and reason for VR's resurrection. Facebook made it clear that the acquisition of Oculus was part of a 10+ year timeline to build the next computing platform. Eying the success of Google with Android and Microsoft with Windows, they used their newfound tech-oligopoly status to invest heavily in VR. Other companies followed with their own VR or AR investments, but the Facebook investment guaranteed that the hardware would continue to improve for the foreseeable future.

After six years we've weathered the boom and bust of the Gartner Hype Cycle and seen multiple generations of hardware and software improvements. On the hardware side, we now have fully untethered 6-degree-of-freedom (6DOF) devices.

What is 6DOF? To review, it's your ability to move your head and hands in physical space. 3DOF means you can only rotate, which feels unnatural and makes many people sick because your brain thinks you should be moving but the picture in the headset doesn't change to match.

What is standalone? VR devices require a lot of compute power, and previously required external sensors to track your movement. Standalone devices have a mobile computer in the headset, and use cameras + clever algorithms to track your head and hand movements. Before you required an expensive (and often heavy) computer and had to set up sensors in your specified play-space. With standalone, you just pick up your headset and can use it immediately anywhere.

So, the hardware is now ready and affordable for both consumers and enterprises. How about the software?

Since VR's resurrection, we've seen adopters in industry such as car companies and architecture firms. Both of these industries have been fast adopters of VR, gaining massive productivity savings and qualitative boosts. Medical and military have also seen amazing cost savings, since those two industries have been using VR for decades! However, the scale of VR use in these industries and the amount of useful software has grown tremendously.

I highlight these industries because they've already been using VR and seeing a large bottom-line benefit without the 2020 VR hardware. The benefits were so large that despite the friction of price, setup, and use, they used VR anyway. Now, many of those barriers have been removed, so much so that thousands of industries stand to benefit from VR standalone adoption.

Since 2014, the industry has learned a plethora of tricks to prevent simulator sickness, and 3D engines used to develop applications have increased their rendering performance. The result is that a developer today can create a comfortable experience on standalone hardware, as long as they keep certain performance considerations in mind. On the consumer end, we've seen several "killer apps" that are impossible without VR, such as Beat Saber and Echo Arena.

When Oculus stated the moniker "VR is Now" at their 2019 keynote, it wasn't simply a piece of marketing voodoo. Because of the current hardware and software ecosystem of VR, there are thousands of enterprise use-cases that could be built TODAY that would have a measurable business impact. Scalable, more effective training is a big one, and one of my primary focuses, but there are a plethora of practical uses. On the consumer side, there is finally a device with ease of use and price point that "just works". These first six years of

VR have been a wild ride of growth and exploration. These next six will see more widespread adoption and practical use.

In 15 years we'll likely use VR / AR as our primary computing device in the workplace, but with the hardware available NOW, VR will be an extremely useful tool for businesses and a fun mobile console for consumers.

AR is Coming

While VR is ready to start garnering mass adoption, AR is still in the early-adopters phase. The tech for AR headsets isn't consumer ready, but for some businesses its jankiness is outweighed by the need for unique solutions.

The good news is that AR hardware will continue to improve. I would be surprised if Facebook didn't release an AR system to compete with whatever Apple ends up releasing. Microsoft is already continually iterating on a released enterprise AR device (Hololens and Hololens 2), and there are several startups releasing tech in the space (Magic Leap and Nreal being the main ones). Although a number of startups have died along the way (Meta and ODG among some of the better known companies), AR hardware continues to improve. The stakes are high, since a compelling consumer AR HMD could be as large a product category as smartphones.

Speaking of which, many smartphones and tablets (both iOS and Android) now support handheld AR. Although the use cases of handheld AR are more limited, the devices are cheaper and already in the hands of millions of people.

Which Hardware Should I Use?

VR / AR hardware is rapidly evolving. Because of this, some of the specific hardware in this section will become outdated within a few years. To combat this, I've organized my hardware recommendations by category. These broad general categories (VR vs AR, Standalone vs Tethered, 6DOF vs 3DOF) should stand the test of time more effectively. So, if you're reading this in 2022 or later, I'd recommend looking up the current hardware for the category that seems to fit your use case best.

If you already have a strong understanding of VR / AR hardware you can skip to the Afterword, but otherwise this and the "Advantages of VR / AR" chapter are a pair for helping you determine which XR hardware + software combination will help your business most.

Tethered 6DOF VR

The highest fidelity immersive experience possible is achieved by a VR headset connected to a powerful computer. 6DOF tracking allows you to move naturally and comfortably (i.e. no sim sickness) within VR. A computer with a powerful CPU and GPU processor allows higher frame rates and higher resolution rendering, as well as increased software complexity. The power drawn from an external source means the headset stays cooler, and can draw power indefinitely in much larger quantities than is possible on mobile.

Most VR headsets use a cable to connect to their computer, but wireless transmission is possible, albeit with bulky add-ons. Backpack computers have also become a popular solution for situations where high-fidelity with larger play areas are needed (such as warehouse scale VR arcades).

To give you an idea of the computational advantages of connecting to a computer rather than using standalone hardware, the recommended minimum specification computer hardware for tethered VR allows about 10x the software processing budget. With more powerful hardware, which is easy to customize with an external computer, you can go even further.

As of 2020, only computers running the Windows operating system (OS) work first-party with tethered VR headsets (except the Playstation VR, which I wouldn't recommend for businesses). The Linux OS is in the early stages of VR support, but I would recommend staying away from it unless you really know what you are doing.

A minimum spec (specification) VR-ready PC (personal computer) costs about $600 as of early 2020, which is quite a bit lower than what it used to cost just three years ago ($1000+). Because of the slowdown of Moore's Law (which predicted the doubling of transistors on a chip every two years), it's hard to predict what kind of further price drop we'll see. That said, this is the pricing for bare-minimum spec hardware, not recommended hardware. Chances are you'll want computers beefier than the minimum if you've decided to go with tethered VR.

I recommend looking up the current minimum computer specs of whatever headset you decide to use, and ideally purchasing something more powerful. Also keep in mind that there are laptops on the market that can run VR if you need something powerful but still semi-mobile. The best performance will always be a desktop computer though, because of heat, power draw, and more room for beefy hardware. Investing in good cooling hardware can also make a huge difference in performance (I personally use liquid cooling in my own desktop computer).

Considerations

So, why should you use a tethered PC VR headset? Well, first you have to determine whether you need VR or AR. If your use case doesn't require interacting with things in the physical environment, VR is the better choice since it offers total control and the hardware is further along.

To be clear, VR can simulate a lot of interactions, making a user feel like they are in a physical environment. You should only choose AR if the interactions in the physical world can't be simulated to a sufficient degree. For example, an oil rig training app might decide to use VR because it can simulate being on the rig without having to go there. Even hand motions like turning a valve or pressing buttons can be included to a fairly high fidelity. However, the oil rig company may decide it's very important that trainees get practice turning the actual valves since they can get slippery. In that case they may decide to use AR with a physical training course, or on the oil rig itself. Alternatively, they may use a combination of VR with physical training.

Once you've decided to use VR, the next question is 6DOF vs 3DOF. If you're only using 180 or 360 degree stereoscopic or flat videos, then 6DOF is unnecessary. Otherwise, you're better off with 6DOF as it's more comfortable and has more possibilities.

Finally, tethered vs untethered. The first major consideration for this is how much processing power your app will need. An untethered headset is ultimately limited in how much compute it has, while a tethered headset has massively more compute and that compute can be variable.

3D modeling is a great example of a use case that benefits from a tethered experience. Modeling can get computationally expensive very quickly, and an external PC is pretty much necessary to allow professional VR modelling at this time. You'll need to think about the complexity of your use case needs, and likely want to consult a developer. Many use cases can be made mobile with enough effort, but some lose a lot to the experience or simply can't do the job.

Your second major consideration is how much mobility you need. I've lugged two different desktop PC's plus monitors across the United States, as well as a VR laptop and headset half-way around the world. It's a lot of luggage to travel with, and as soon as you start adding the need for more than one headset it goes from a logistic hurdle to a logistical nightmare. So, if your headsets are mostly staying in one place you're fine with tethered, but if you're going to be moving them around often, standalone is probably better.

Setup and operation for tethered headsets is also more complex than standalones. For a PC connected headset you have to make sure the PC drivers and VR software are downloaded and updated, and some tethered headsets require external sensor setups. You'd also be surprised how often someone's "not working" VR headset just has a cable or two that aren't plugged in. Standalones just work when you turn them on (assuming their battery is charged).

If your use case requires hours on end of operation, tethered headsets can accomplish this, while standalone headsets run on battery and would need to be swapped out. Technically you could use a standalone headset while it is plugged in to charge, but they're not designed for this.

Tethered VR headsets basically require that you develop your app on a computer running Windows (since otherwise you can't test your app as you develop it). In contrast, since standalone devices generally run on a version of Android you can develop apps on a Mac, Linux, or Windows computer then transfer the app to the headset to test.

It's also worth noting that tethered VR headsets generally have higher refresh rates and better tracking quality than standalone, so if user comfort and immersion is your sole concern tethered will be better. For the same reason (i.e. higher processing and electric power) there are options for tethered headsets with better resolutions than you can find on standalone. If image clarity (such as reading lots of text) is important to your use case, tethered has the potential to offer advantages.

The Headsets

If you don't mind setting up external sensors, devices like the Valve Index or HTC Vive can offer the highest-quality tracking. They use "base stations" mounted in the corners of your "play space" to shoot invisible-to-the-eye lasers at your headset, which then senses the lasers and positions itself.

Most other tethered headsets nowadays are opting for an inside-out tracking approach, using cameras on the headset to track the headset's movement and rotation through space (in addition to the other traditional sensors such as accelerometer and gyroscope). The Oculus Rift S, Vive Cosmos, and Windows Mixed Reality headsets use this approach. The obvious advantage of this is that when you plug the headset into the computer you immediately have 360 degree 6DOF tracking without the need for setting up any sensors.

All of these tethered headsets use 6DOF and come with two 6DOF hand controllers, so your decision making comes down to cost, desired fidelity, setup complexity, and extra features. For example, there are a number of headset startups that are offering tethered VR headsets with higher resolutions and field of view. I won't name them because I personally wouldn't recommend them and many will likely go bankrupt in a few years. Having said that, if those features are a priority for your use case the options exist.

Personally, within the tethered category I'd recommend the Oculus Rift S or Vive Cosmos for businesses because of their balance of easy setup, low cost, and quality compared to other inside-out headsets. The Windows Mixed reality headsets are the least popular among consumers in the category, and personally I find their quality to be sub-par.

On the more expensive end, the Valve Index is currently the best headset when it comes to overall fidelity. Its controllers offer the ability for finger tracking to a high degree, its external sensor tracking is more reliable than inside-out, and it's capable of 120 Hz refresh rate compared to the Rift S 80Hz and Vive Cosmos 90Hz. If you need eye-tracking, the HTC Vive (not to be confused with the Cosmos) has a variant that supports that, and the HTC Vive offerings have good quality overall.

Standalone 6DOF VR

Okay, so you've chosen VR. You want a high-quality user experience that can transport you into any 3D scenario. In the majority of cases, a 6DOF standalone headset will be the best choice for your business.

Considerations

With an untethered (i.e. standalone) 6DOF headset, you have full freedom to use VR with 360 degrees in any indoor environment. The inside-out camera tracking requires there to be features to track, so tracking breaks down when out in the open sky or in a featureless (i.e. blank walls no furniture) room. Mirrors can also cause tracking issues. That said, the inside-out tracking is quite resilient except in those cases.

Because standalone devices are self-contained, you simply turn them on and they work. The only setup (if any) is a prompted drawing or confirmation of your safety bounds. All 6DOF VR headsets employ a grid that pops up when you approach the edge of your pre-set safe space (so that you don't run into walls or furniture while using them). Since you can use standalone VR basically anywhere, devices like the Oculus Quest allow you to see through to the physical world via cameras, and have you easily draw an area of safe movement (which gets saved for if you use the VR device in the same room another day). This drawing can be skipped in favour of a seated / standing bounds option that makes your play space a circle around you. Some standalone headsets default to this option.

Because standalone devices run a custom operating system, usually based on Android, the headset should always work as long as it's charged. System updates can be postponed until a more convenient time (or indefinitely), so you can have the confidence that whenever you go to use your VR software, you can use it right away.

Without the need for an external computer, portability is easier. If you're shipping headsets to customers, this means cheaper shipping costs. Additionally, there's no need for any customer setup upon receiving the headset (other than to mark safety bounds). Even if you're not shipping headsets but need them to move between rooms or to travel with you, standalone makes this much easier.

One of VR's major pain points is the friction of getting a headset on. Standalone makes this as easy as possible by allowing you to simply turn on the headset and start using it. In contrast, tethered headsets have multiple additional friction points. Is the headset plugged in? Is the computer on? Is the software updated? If applicable, are the sensors set up and configured correctly? Have the safety bounds been configured?

As we discussed in the tethered section, standalone devices are not without their weaknesses. They are battery powered, meaning that after a couple hours using the device you'll need to either stop using it or use it while it is plugged in to charge (which is not recommended).

The mobile processors on the headset mean that software created for it have to be well optimized or you risk dropping frames (or *gasp* running consistently below framerate). Performance constraints might translate to lower quality visuals or simulations depending on your situation.

Because the computer is on the headset, standalone devices are also heavier on the head than their tethered counterparts. Combined with reduced refresh rate compared to tethered headsets, more heat, and slightly worse tracking, standalone devices can offer a less comfortable and lower fidelity experience than tethered headsets.

Despite these weaknesses, VR standalone is a game changer for many businesses. The leading standalones on the market offer a good enough experience fidelity for sim sickness to be avoided and users to feel immersed. All this at a price point that is affordable for businesses.

The Headsets

The Oculus Quest and Vive Focus (Plus) are the leading standalone VR headsets as of the time of this writing. Really, the Oculus Quest is unparalleled in terms of its sleekness, tracking quality, and user experience.

The Oculus Quest comes with a headset and two 6DOF controllers that are tracked by the cameras on the headset. The headset also supports direct hand tracking, which can be used as an alternative input to the controllers. As of early 2020 this is an experimental feature, and there are certain issues with camera-based hand tracking such as occlusion (i.e. hands blocking each other) that prevent the system from being perfect. However, I believe hand tracking based input will be great for situations where you want to simplify even further, requiring only the headset and not needing to teach the controllers.

Vive Focus is a 6DOF headset with a 3DOF controller. Vive Focus Plus replaces the 3DOF controller with two 6DOF ones. Although I'm very bullish on Quest and Facebook's longevity (compared to a struggling HTC), the Vive Focus Plus is another option for businesses.

When using the Quest and Vive Focus for business purposes, you are required to buy a yearly subscription for each headset (~$200 per year), which comes with warranty repair and other business features.

New standalones will continue to be released, so although I doubt anything will dethrone the Quest, do keep an eye out. The Pico Neo 2 headset is a standalone that offers increased display resolution and controllers that use magnetism, so theoretically you don't lose hand tracking when the controllers are out of sight of the headset. The Neo 2 also has a variant that includes built-in eye tracking. I haven't tried the headset, and there's a chance the headset will be irrelevant in a few years (by being outcompeted, etc), but I thought it was neat enough to mention and a good example of continued innovation and headset customizability in the space.

A last point to consider is that since standalones have offerings that specifically target businesses, there are useful-to-business features like kiosk mode available from the headset makers. Kiosk mode makes it so that you can only use specified apps in the headset. For tethered VR this is harder to achieve and generally requires custom software. There are also enterprise features such as remote software deployment and updates to all your headsets.

Standalone 3DOF VR

3DOF VR (rotation tracking only) may cease to be a product category some day. Its biggest advantage is lower cost, but the declining cost of 6DOF headsets means no-sim-sickness VR is becoming more and more affordable.

Considerations

At this point, there are no 3DOF tethered VR headsets worth using on the market (the first Oculus Developer Kit released in 2013 was tethered 3DOF, but 6DOF was added to the Dev Kit 2 in 2014). So, we can assume that if you're talking about 3DOF VR hardware, it's standalone.

If you're using VR to portray physical world 180 or 360 degree video, 3DOF VR is all you need. Video based VR can be useful for situations where you want to transport someone into a physical world situation as an observer. You can get away with spending less money on each headset since you'll not be making use of the 6DOF capabilities.

Once the upfront cost of the camera rig is paid for, VR video capture *can* be relatively cheap to produce compared to 3D hand created art and programming. Several companies already have platforms built that streamline the creation of VR video experiences, even adding simple interactivity such as quiz questions.

For example, insurance agents training to recognize different types of damage at a physical "training house" can have a VR video that takes them to that house whenever they want. The cost of flying agents to the house is considerable, and there is a limit to how many people can be in the house training at once, so this VR video training can provide a lot of value as either a replacement or follow-up supplement to increase learning retention.

VR video is not always easier and cheaper than 3D counterparts. Depending on the scenario, you may have to pay actors, lighting and sound crew, and other roles associated with recording live video. Unlike content that is in a 3D engine, video requires that scheduling all be aligned. If later in editing something is missing, or you want to make changes, it can be expensive to book another shoot. 3D engine content, in contrast, can be edited and changed asynchronously. With video you are stuck with whatever footage you shoot, while with 3D engine content you can edit anything as the need arises.

Another small advantage of 3DOF VR headsets is that there's zero setup. Because you can't move with the headset on, there is no guardian safety bounds system to configure.

In addition to VR video, 3DOF headsets can also be okay for watching traditional 2D media. You can watch video content on a large virtual monitor, including in stereoscopic 3D. At this point your VR headset would essentially become a wearable 3D TV. For consumers, this use of VR as a larger portable virtual monitor is actually one of the most popular uses of the headsets. Although I doubt this use case alone would be a good reason for businesses to buy VR, it is a side consideration (6DOF headsets can accomplish this more comfortably).

The Headsets

As of early 2020, the Oculus Go is the best 3DOF VR standalone device on the market. There are also a number of Chinese 3DOF headsets (I can't speak to their quality as I haven't tried them). If you live in the US and want 3DOF standalone, go with the Go.

What about Google Cardboard, or other phone-powered VR headsets? Oculus and Samsung discontinued the Samsung Gear VR, and Google discontinued its Daydream headsets. Phone powered VR falls in a gray zone of tethered 3DOF VR, but I'm including it here because, quite simply, the category is becoming obsolete. On the low end, cheap headsets like the Google Cardboard offered some semblance of a VR experience, but were quite far from the experience possible on higher end headsets. The high end phone powered headsets like Gear VR gave an experience similar to the Oculus Go, but at the cost of quickly draining your phone battery and requiring you to mount the phone, creating a high friction of use.

I would highly recommend NOT using phone powered 3DOF VR for enterprise. The only exception to this would be if you had zero budget for a classroom full of people, and were using VR as a gimmick for spurring imagination (i.e. Google Expeditions, which brought Google Cardboard to classrooms around the US for "virtual field trips").

In terms of 3DOF interactivity, you can expect a range from a single button to press (or in some cases swipe) to a 3DOF controller (which can serve decently as a laser pointer).

Keep in mind that 6DOF headsets can do everything a 3DOF headset can do and more, so if you're looking to maximize your optionality and headset longevity, stay away from 3DOF.

AR Head Mounted Displays (HMDs)

So, you've done the research and for one reason or another, you need to see the physical and digital worlds at the same time. Maybe you're building furniture and need the user to see what they're building as well as AR instructions. Perhaps you're creating contextual information around a massive theme park. Whatever the use, AR will help you bring digital elements into the physical world.

Considerations

Head mounted AR is going to be best in situations where you want a user to be able to move naturally, especially if they need both hands for virtual and physical interaction. Because the display's field of view matches where you are looking, there's no need to consciously angle a device at the area you want AR visuals.

AR HMDs are specialized hardware, meaning you know the headsets will be optimized for AR use (compared to smartphones which can do many more things and may make hardware trade-offs that don't maximize the AR experience).

Most AR headsets can generate a 3D mesh matching the physical objects in your environment. This mesh is useful for things like tables, chairs, and walls but doesn't work well for objects that move (although who's to say what future machine learning breakthroughs will make possible).

AR HMDs have varied costs, but tend to be on the more expensive side (compared to handheld AR). Like VR headsets, they experience reduced quality in outdoor lighting scenarios. If it's too dark or too bright the tracking quality is reduced, and in bright environments the screen visuals can appear faded in comparison to the physical world.

The Hardware

The Hololens 2 is probably the best AR HMD for businesses that can afford its price. The device is a creation of Microsoft, and built on the success of the Hololens 1 developer kit (which was released in 2016). The device is exclusively targeted at businesses, and Microsoft has a lot of experience supporting business customers. As of early 2020 the device costs $3,500.

The Magic Leap 1 is another option ($2300 as of early 2020, although the enterprise version brings the cost up to $3000). The device was created by Magic Leap, an AR startup that raised $2.6 billion as of early 2020. Only time will tell if Magic Leap can create an AR device to compete with the tech giants or whether they'll run out of funding. Their first device, the Magic Leap 1, is solid quality for an AR device.

Nreal is a Chinese startup company that's creating AR glasses at the least expensive price. As of early 2020 they sell a developer kit for $1100 and enterprise edition for $2000 (their debut device is called the Nreal Light). They claim they'll release a $500 consumer device this year. The effective price may be greater because the Nreal Light requires a smartphone to power it. Although the Nreal quality is the lowest of these three AR headsets (their 6DOF tracking is substantially worse and the form factor falls off many peoples faces), this may change over time. The Nreal Light's form factor is the smallest of these AR HMDs, and looks the most like regular glasses.

At the end of the day, which AR headset to use comes down to a tradeoff between desired fidelity and cost per headset. Hololens 2 is a standalone device with the best optical finger tracking input. Magic Leap 1 has a 6DOF controller with some latency as well as hand tracking (albeit Microsoft's hand tracking is much better). The Magic Leap 1 is a smaller form factor than the Hololens, but is tethered to a custom round computer (about hand sized) that you must mount on your pocket. Nreal is powered by your smartphone, which can act as a controller (or you can use the provided 3DOF controller).

All these devices have eye tracking and a microphone, so can use those as input methods (to different degrees of quality). Note, the early 2020 version of Nreal Light doesn't include eye tracking, but the company claims its release version will. With these three AR headsets, the price differences really correspond to differences in quality (unlike in VR where devices are closer in price and sometimes the cheaper devices are better).

Remember, AR is still in its early stages, so I'd advise you to look up the latest AR headset features on their product websites (as well as see if there are any new headsets not mentioned here). For example, as of the time of this writing Nreal's headset has not fully launched. If you want something that you know will have support for years to come, Microsoft Hololens 2 is your best bet (with the better quality being a bonus), but if its price is too high there are other options.

Handheld AR

If you want mixing of physical and digital worlds but are trying to save money, utilize people's existing devices, or give people an experience they are more familiar with, handheld AR can be a useful tool.

Considerations

The biggest advantages of handheld AR devices are that they're cheaper and relatively widespread. If you are purely distributing software and not providing the hardware, handheld AR can be the way to go. For example, some companies have started providing AR apps that help purchasers build complicated products, such as child play gyms.

Another example use of handheld AR that takes advantage of their cheaper price and ubiquity is an app that helps you visualize Wifi strength within a physical space. If you're arming your IT people or event coordinators with such a software, buying a headset is probably going overboard. Instead, let them use their own smartphone or buy them an AR enabled smartphone, which is a cheaper option.

The biggest downside to handheld AR is that you can only use it one handed, and the interactions are constrained to your touch screen rather than interacting directly with virtual objects. You also have to use some of your concentration to keep the phone pointed at what you want to look at, making it a less effective learning tool than head mounted AR since aiming the phone uses more working memory.

Handheld AR suffers all the same issues as head mounted AR in regards to lighting and tracking software (such as mesh generation).

The Hardware

There are many options available for handheld AR. Just check to make sure the device you are purchasing supports ARKit (iOS) or ARCore (Android). As additional consideration, more powerful smartphones and tablets will have better AR performance (and AR takes a lot of processing power). Camera quality can also make a difference for tracking quality and the visual quality of the physical-world displayed on screen. Display quality will affect the visuals of both the virtual and physical elements.

Almost every year we're seeing the introduction of new sensors and cameras on smartphones. High end smartphones have started adding depth sensors (this is what allows you to unlock your iPhone by showing your face). As of early 2020 most of these smartphones put the depth sensors on the front of the phone, which is useful for AR that interacts with your face (such as Snapchat filters that turn you into a kitten or any number of crazy things in real time). However, depth sensors will likely be added to the backs of some smartphones for AR use (such as scanning of physical world objects into 3D models). Of course, other tech may be used for this instead, such as machine learning enabled computer vision.

Generally, the more you pay for the smartphone, the better the AR experience will be, unless you see the phone has specific sensors (such as depth sensors) that are targeting AR.

Peripherals

You may decide you need extra hardware beyond just the VR / AR device. If this is the case, you can often get what you need custom built, as long as you have the budget. Some peripherals such as a tracked baseball bat or two handed gun can be obtained fairly inexpensively. For instance, HTC makes mountable tracking pucks that work with their SteamVR tracking system for $99 a piece. Other peripherals, such as a moving flight simulation chair, can cost $50,000.

If you need peripherals, my recommendation is to do an internet search for what you're looking for (there may be a company that already manufactures what you need) and if that doesn't work for your application, consult a VR / AR hardware professional.

Future Hardware

Current VR and AR hardware is impressive, but it's not a perfect re-creation of reality. We are still many years away from an XR system where you can't tell the difference between the virtual and physical worlds. Without even going high sci-fi, there are a number of shortcomings of the current tech that if fixed would provide immediate benefit. In this section I'll explain some of the most promising XR tech improvements that we'll likely see within the next 15 years, many of which we'll probably see long before then.

Varifocal

Current XR displays have only one or two focal points. If you think about the mechanics of a VR headset, your eyes are looking through a lens at a display. That display has a fixed position, and all the visuals on it are made to appear 3D and to have infinite depth. However, your eyes can only properly focus on the screen position. For most headsets this focal point is around 2 meters away, meaning that visuals displayed at that distance from you in the virtual world will appear the most clear.

If you try to focus on visuals at other depths, you run into Vergence Accommodation Conflict. Quite simply, Vergence Accommodation Conflict is a mismatch between the apparent distance of an object you want to focus on, and the actual distance of the visual. In XR if you look at a tree 10 meters away, your eyes are focusing way past the position of the screen, but the screen is still only 2 meters away. This can result in eye strain and headaches, as well as blurred visuals. This is perhaps the greatest XR hardware comfort issue remaining.

The potential solution to Vergence Accommodation Conflict is to use a display with variable focal distances (known as varifocal). Facebook (Oculus) Reality Labs has shown off research of functioning varifocal VR display systems and as of early 2020 were working on their third iteration of a headset under the code name Half Dome. Essentially, varifocal headsets use eye tracking to determine where you are focusing. Then they move the focal distance of the display dynamically based on that.

The first two Half Dome prototypes did this by physically moving the lens. Their third system uses an electronic system instead, turning different lenses in a stack on or off depending on the desired focal distance. Whatever solution ends up working well enough to be included in a release product is unknown, but varifocal will likely become the norm someday.

Eye Tracking

Eye tracking (i.e. tracking where you are looking) is interesting because in addition to being useful on its own, it's an enabling technology for things like varifocal displays and foveated rendering (which we'll talk about later). Many AR headsets already include eye tracking, so for those I'd expect the hardware and especially the software to improve in the future. Eye tracking is currently pretty good, but it will continue to get better.

Some VR headsets can already be purchased that include eye tracking. As the years progress I think it's likely we'll see eye tracking included in more VR headsets, but the inclusion will probably be tied to the other technologies that eye tracking enables.

For standalone headsets especially, you have to make trade-offs. Eye tracking is an additional processing and power draw, and adds weight via the necessary cameras. Advances in batteries, cameras, computer chips, and eye tracking software efficiency may lessen the burden.

Facial Tracking

Being able to see facial expressions remotely is a big reason for why video conferencing became popular. Facial expressions provide a higher communication bandwidth, allowing you to intuit the effects of your conversation on the person you're talking to, and allowing for subtle cues (such as the opening of your mouth indicating "I'm about to start speaking" so that you don't talk over each other).

I think it's likely that facial tracking (i.e. cameras and software that track your facial movement) will be included in XR headsets in the future. I've already seen a few prototypes of facial tracking systems on VR headsets. Additionally, things like Snapchat filters and iPhone Animojis show that the software for tracking facial movement has come a long way.

Social interaction without facial expression in VR and AR is still useful, but with facial tracking (and potentially the addition of eye tracking), that social interaction can become almost as high bandwidth as in-person interaction.

Full Hand Tracking

The ability to use our full hands in XR has long been sought after. Headsets like the Hololens 2 use it as its primary input method, while the Oculus Quest offers it as a secondary input modality

The main method of full hand tracking utilized in available products is optical. That is, cameras or other sensors mounted on a headset sense your hands in a certain area in front of you. The main issue with this is that your hands can block each other, or even themselves (if you face your fingers away from you at an angle, you can't see your fingers moving). Other objects can also get in the way of the sensors. This issue is known as occlusion. The software can try to guess, and clever sensor placement can mitigate this somewhat, but head-mounted optical systems will likely always suffer from occlusion issues.

Another issue with head-mounted optical systems is that there's a box of area where the hands are tracked, and moving the hands out of the area degrades and eventually drops tracking. Depending on the size and placement of that box, you may lose tracking often or have to move your hands to positions that are tiring over time.

Finally, if your hand tracking is purely optical there is no touch feedback for interactions (known as haptic feedback). Touch is a very useful sense for precision and immersion, and this is impossible to achieve with a purely head mounted optical system. Technically you can make use of "self-haptics" such as touching your fingers together, but this is unable to respond to the virtual environment and can feel uncomfortable with repeated use.

Interestingly, the Valve Index VR headset includes a controller based hand tracking system that fixes all of these issues (at the cost of being less portable and self contained). The Index's "knuckles" controllers strap onto your hands, using external sensors to track the hand in 6DOF and sensors on the controller to track your fingers (in addition to providing buttons and haptic feedback).

Moving towards the future, it's possible we'll see other solutions that creatively blend controllers and hands. For example Facebook recently acquired CTRL-Labs, which was building an arm band that monitored the signals your brain sent to your hand. If they get the tech working well enough, I could imagine dual wrist-bands tracked in 6DOF by the headset with full finger tracking. It may even be possible to "write" haptics signals, or at the very least provide micro haptics on the armband that allow you to remap touch feedback. We remap inputs all the time, such as when we move a mouse on a 2D horizontal plane but it actually moves on a vertical one.

Another solution seen in labs is the use of gloves that track the positions of the fingers, and which in theory can provide touch feedback. According to Facebook such a system can allow very precise hand tracking, but it's unclear whether a glove system will ever make it out of the lab. Gloves are difficult to productize because everyone has different hand sizes, leading to a more expensive product, and putting gloves on and off is higher friction than picking up a controller. Gloves are also harder to clean, especially if they have electronics in them.

On the design side, we're at the very beginning of figuring out how to design user interfaces with accurate hand tracking, and the level of that accuracy dictates how we design. For example, the Quest hand tracking is not very precise (relatively) and can suffer occlusion, so user experience design (UX) has to take that into account. An early Oculus UX prototype had users using a hand-based menu, but found that people kept occluding their hands with each other while trying to use it. With a precise system like Facebook Reality Labs' gloves, this would not be an issue.

Body Tracking

Ubiquitous body tracking at a consumer level is probably a long way off. The cheapest way to add body tracking to current (early 2020) VR hardware is to buy Vive tracking pucks, which at $99 each will set you back about $300 (one tracker for each foot and one for your waist). This is assuming you already have a SteamVR headset (such as a Vive or Index) and its external lighthouse sensors. Still, this is impressive and definitely within the realm of affordable for businesses should you need leg and body positions. Even in the consumer space there's a community of people who use this full body tracking for social games like VRchat.

In comparison, professional motion capture suits range from about $2,000 to $10,000. These suits are IMU (Inertial Measurement Unit) based, meaning they don't require external sensors but can suffer some drift. Optical based motion capture can get even pricier or about the same depending on your desired level of fidelity. The advantages of professional motion capture (often referred to as mocap) are that you get way more tracked points for a more accurate capture of a person's exact movement. In comparison, tracking only six points (like with the SteamVR system) means there is a lot of software interpolation about how parts of your body are moving.

One of the most important of these interpolations is inverse kinematics. For body movement, inverse kinematics is the maintaining of realistic joint movements. If you move your hand, your elbow and arm should move in certain ways accordingly. With good inverse kinematics, your estimated arm and elbow positions will match their actual positions most of the time. It won't always match when you have only six position inputs because there are often multiple possible solves for any given position, but a good system will show something plausible. Inverse kinematics with limited tracked points is already pretty good, but will continue to improve.

Looking to the future, machine learning advances may some day allow very accurate optical full body capture for a low price. Algorithms trained to recognize people's bodies from a video already exist in an early form. Full body capture may one day be as simple as setting up one or two cameras.

Haptics

The main form of touch currently available in XR comes in the form of rumbling controllers. This can be surprisingly helpful for feedback within the virtual world. However, it's not the same as actually touching virtual objects.

A number of labs and companies have been working to try to bring more nuanced touch to our virtual worlds. For example, a team at the University of Melbourne developed some haptic gloves that used machine learning to predict likely touch events (reducing latency). Haptic gloves generally provide some form of force feedback, so that when you pick up a virtual ball, your hand actually stops as if the ball was solid. For uses such as remote surgery, low latency haptics could be useful for increasing precision.

The good news is that if you desperately need more accurate haptics, you'll probably be able to get some devices relatively soon (for example, HaptX is a company that as of early 2020 has a development kit). Unfortunately, the glove haptics devices in the works are very bulky and will probably remain expensive. The quality of the haptics also has a way to go to feel fully realistic.

Other approaches include using ultrasound to project touchable holograms. A company called Ultraleap uses this for things like providing haptic feedback on car dashboards. It's unclear if this will ever find a use for head mounted XR, but it's interesting. This kind of haptics is incapable of fully stopping your hands' movements, however, so is more of a "rumble in air".

Better Fundamentals

Resolution of displays will continue to increase. Even the current VR displays are below the pixels-per-inch we're used to with 1080p monitors (with VR headsets you have to measure pixels per inch since the lenses magnify the pixels). If you need higher resolution today, you can probably get it from specialized headset vendors, but the overall display quality should go up over time. In just three years the Oculus Rift resolution jumped from 2160 x 1200 to 2560 x 1440.

AR displays already have a relatively high resolution because the field of view is so much smaller. Since small field of view is still a weakness of AR HMDs, resolution will need to increase along with any increases of field of view to maintain display quality.

Refresh rates may actually stagnate around an "acceptable level" that doesn't make most people sick for a little while (due to performance considerations), but eventually refresh rates should go up as well. In 2016 90 Hz was the fastest you could get, and about three years later the Valve Index launched with the ability for 120 Hz. The Rift S actually went backwards from 90 Hz to 80 Hz, but I hope this isn't a trend that will continue. Although I don't expect to see a 1000 Hz XR display in any kind of product for a very long while, who knows what is possible?

Field of view around 110 degrees seems to be fine for now. You can become immersed in VR to the point where you forget you are wearing a headset. That field of view may increase over time, but it will probably do so slowly in the mass market headsets. You can get a larger field of view in some headsets today, but at a reduction in other qualities. Since increases to field of view will mostly only affect your peripheral vision, we may see more headsets with lower resolution at the edges of the display.

AR headsets in contrast have an inadequate field of view (FOV) to cause much presence. You view your virtual holograms through a window. The Hololens 2 has an approximate 57 degree diagonal FOV which is a big jump from the first Hololens' 34 degree FOV. AR FOV should continue to increase until it reaches a point like VR that allows full immersion.

6DOF tracking quality will also continue to improve, especially for inside-out devices (i.e. devices that track themselves in any room with sensors on the device). Much of the SLAM tracking done so far doesn't use machine learning, but as computer vision AI algorithms improve they may end up becoming the norm.

Increases in computer processing power will also improve these fundamental XR technologies. With the slowdown of Moore's Law, I'd expect to see improvements in the form of specialized processors that are optimized for certain tasks, as well as cooling improvements from material science and design. Hopefully we'll achieve another computing breakthrough (such as graphene chips) at some point in the future, which will allow the inclusion of all these improvements without tradeoffs. However, breakthroughs are hard to predict.

Even without any processor breakthroughs, software optimizations and possibly machine learning can take us far. On top of that, data transfer improvements may allow remote rendering, so the computer you run the XR device on could be in a nearby datacenter. Tech like 5G and other networking improvements may enable lightweight XR devices with very high simulation quality. Gaming products like Google Stadia and Nvidia Geforce Now already allow streaming of online games (albeit at a latency too high for VR). It's not hard to believe that at some point in the future our XR could be "cloud" powered.

AI Denoising (Software)

One of the most interesting advances we're seeing in the realm of rendering is the use of machine learning to generate imagery. Probably the most popular example of this is "style transfer", a class of machine learning algorithms trained to take a picture and put its style (such as color and line work) onto another picture or video. Want your cat to look like it's made of pizza? Feed the cat and pizza pictures into the algorithm and your pizza cat is delivered.

More fundamentally useful machine learning algorithms are now on the cusp. One example of this is the use of machine learning to denoise high quality images. If you've ever taken a picture in poor lighting and your picture was all grainy, that's a noisy image. Machine learning algorithms can take that image and generate a version that looks clear and high quality by filling in a best guess of how the picture should look.

For XR this could be very useful, because rather than rendering full resolution for a high definition display, you can render a fraction of the frame's image and let the AI algorithm fill in the rest of the image. As these algorithms improve and get more efficient, they may provide a way to render better imagery at a fraction of the compute cost.

Foveated Rendering (Software + Hardware)

A related technique to AI denoising is foveated rendering, which is the displaying of lower quality imagery at the periphery of your vision. The area where we can focus our attention (and with it our detailed vision) is fairly small, so it seems like a waste to render the entire display at high resolution. On an XR headset with eye tracking you could make it so that high resolution is only displayed where you're looking. Meanwhile, the peripheral vision can render at lower quality since we can't see the detail anyway.

Facebook Reality Labs showed off a working AI assisted foveated rendering system called DeepFovea in late 2019. Using a generative adversarial neural network (a type of machine learning algorithm), they were able to generate plausible imagery for the peripheral vision, claiming to achieve up to 14x compression on color video. Importantly, this computation savings was achieved without a noticeable image difference to testers.

I expect we'll see foveated rendering deployed at some point before 2025. The performance cost savings are potentially huge if they can be made to work in publicly available and affordable hardware. Also keep in mind that eye tracking is necessary for foveated rendering to make its way into headsets. Luckily most AR headsets already have eye tracking, and eye tracking should make its way into more VR headsets.

Conclusions

The future of XR technology is bright. Already we have devices that trick the brain without causing sim sickness and that are useful. With backing from major tech companies and a large number of startups the tech will continue to advance. Personally I believe we'll use XR devices as our primary computing platform by 2035. The main hurdle for this to become reality is a device you can work in comfortably for hours at a time. Once you can create high definition virtual monitors in a lightweight XR headset with a wide field of view and comfortable framerate, your need for stationary flat monitors greatly decreases since you can put virtual monitors anywhere.

Even without this perfect work device, what we have now allows a range of useful functions that otherwise would be impossible. Luckily, software created with these devices will be relatively easy to support on new hardware. The major 3D engines and SDKs used to build XR content have been built with forward compatibility in mind.

AFTERWORD: SOCIAL RESPONSIBILITY

Regardless of race, religion, or nationality, we must understand that what we do with XR technology will affect us all as a society. XR is a vital piece in the greater puzzle of humanity's challenges. The network of humans that makes up this Earth must cooperate to solve these problems and increase our happiness. If you've read this book, then you are already more knowledgeable about XR than 99% of the human population. When you create, think about what you can do to positively influence the world. In doing so, you will help the network of humans living on this planet, and when the network succeeds, we all win.

Some of our biggest issues right now are greed, lack of cooperation, and outdated societal systems. People within countries must cooperate to improve the world, and countries must cooperate with each other for the world's mutual benefit. The only thing standing in the way of unprecedented progress and happiness is, ultimately, ourselves. The prioritization of pressing issues like climate change and education is extremely important for the creation of a friendly future. XR will be a media driver, making it the perfect place to enable these changes in paradigm. The world is as we make it, and you are an integral part.

If you enjoyed the book, please rate it on Amazon :)

AKNOWLEDGEMENTS

A big thank you to Noel Gray and Randy Neiditch for help copyediting this book. I'd also like to thank Palmer Lucky and all those who worked for the early Oculus team for giving VR a much needed jump start, and with it accelerating investment in the entire XR industry. Last but not least, I'd like to thank all those working in XR who share their knowledge and expertise to improve the industry as a whole.

ABOUT THE AUTHOR

Sky Nite is a writer, developer, designer, and educator who has worked full-time in the XR industry since 2014. His first book, Virtual Reality Insider, sold over 9000 copies and provided an early look at what was possible with VR. In his two years working at UploadVR, Sky built and taught two 8-10 week VR development bootcamps, both of which saw 100% industry placement within a year of students finishing the programs. Some of his students received grants from Oculus for projects built during the course, and built VR tools in conjunction with NASA engineers. He also partnered with Udacity to build 1/4th of their VR Nanodegree, and taught over 200 students at weekend VR development courses that he designed.

After leaving UploadVR, Sky developed and released two VR games on Steam and the Oculus Store (Top Secret and Meme Dragons). He then wrote a sci-fi novel imagining what XR education would look like in 100 years on a spaceship destined for alien first-contact. Coming back to development with renewed vigor, Sky created an open-source VR Dungeons and Dragons app called RoleplayU. Building on the multiplayer technology from that project, he developed a VR education experiment where users learned 38 bias and fallacy concepts through an interactive memory palace, either alone or with peers. In between these highlights Sky developed numerous other VR and AR prototypes.

Since early 2019, Sky has developed several enterprise VR apps for a variety of clients in industries such as training, retail, and health. His company Modu XR (moduxr.com) offers enterprise development and consulting for VR and AR.

You can contact Sky at vrinsider@gmail.com or follow him on Twitter @VRInsider

If you're interested in using XR for your own business he'd be happy to hear from you!

Printed in Great Britain
by Amazon

82376230R00089